The Road to Cooperstown

ALSO BY TOM STANTON

The Final Season

The Road to Cooperstown

*A Father, Two Sons,
and the Journey
of a Lifetime*

• TOM STANTON •

Thomas Dunne Books   St. Martin's Press   New York

Author's note: Some names and details have been changed to protect the privacy of individuals.

THOMAS DUNNE BOOKS.
An imprint of St. Martin's Press.

Photo on page iv courtesy of the National Baseball
Hall of Fame Library, Cooperstown, N.Y.

Photo on page v courtesy of Betty Stanton

Grateful acknowledgment is made for the permission to excerpt from the
following works:

From the song "Cooperstown, The Town Where Baseball Lives," (pg. 1)
words and music by Terry Cashman (ASCAP) copyright © 1982 PKM
Music, c/o Publishers' Licensing Corporation, P.O. Box 5807, Englewood,
N.J. 07631, used by permission. Terry Cashman's baseball songs are available online at www.winthropmedia.com and www.metrostarrecords.com.

The poem "Gaylord" (pg. 113) is reprinted from *Cooperstown Verses:
Poems About Each Hall of Famer* (McFarland & Company, 2001) and is
used with permission of the author, Mark Schraf.

Library of Congress Cataloging-in-Publication Data

Stanton, Tom.
    The road to Cooperstown : a father, two sons, and the journey of a
lifetime / Tom Stanton.—1st ed.
        p. cm.
    ISBN 0-312-30350-5
    1. Stanton, Tom.   2. Baseball fans—United States—Biography.
3. Baseball fans—United States—Family relationships.   4. Baseball—
United States—History.   5. National Baseball Hall of Fame and
Museum.   I. Title.

GV865.S755S72 2003
796.357'092—dc21
[B]
                                                      2003040862
First Edition: June 2003

10   9   8   7   6   5   4   3   2   1

For Taylor, William, and Zachary Stanton,

sons and brothers

Contents

Prologue

There are times when a passion burns so strongly that nothing seems as significant and the things that should matter fade into the shadows, outshone by a hero, a hobby, or a newfound love.

I saw it happen to Laura, who lived across the street and took a sudden interest in horses and filled her bedroom with statues of Appaloosas and palominos and posters of Black Beauty. I saw it happen to a buddy, Ken, who carried his drawings of military planes—Flying Fortresses and Super Sabres and Spitfires—like classified secrets in a canvas-coated, three-ring binder, which made him an easy target in the halls of Melby Junior High. And it happened to me as well, when I was

---

ABOVE: Joseph Stankiewicz, 1935 *(Edward Stankiewicz)*

eleven and baseball pulled my whole life into its orbit, spinning me gloriously into the sport, sending me on a dreamy journey alight with promise and populated with Reggie Jacksons and Tom Seavers and Johnny Benches and, of course, Kalines and Loliches and Hortons. What I wanted most then was to talk baseball, to watch it, to hear it, to read about it, to convert the uninitiated, to fill my hours with all they could hold. In an adult you might call it an obsession. But that's an ugly word for a child's innocent joy.

My dad understood. He had been similarly enraptured in the age of Ruth and Gehrig. He had collected baseball cards as a boy and read books about Ty Cobb and he savored our common passion. "Tommy, you've got a one-track mind," he said.

I grew up hearing him and my uncles talk of Charlie Gehringer and Dizzy Dean and Schoolboy Rowe, who won sixteen straight in 1934, and seeing my older brother Joey play in pickup games at Robert Frost Field. Early on, I got my first glimpse of Tiger Stadium, the ballpark of my youth, a towering, embracing place, a home to heroes, a keeper of dreams. Our team won it all that year, in 1968, denying Lou Brock and Bob Gibson a third World Series title. It was the beginning for me, and to be entirely forthright I remember little of it, save for the celebration afterward: beeping horns, toilet paper in the trees, hooting and howling in the streets. Many of the players who shared in that summer went on to become my idols, their legend not just lingering but growing larger.

The winter after that joyous 1971 World Series in which Clemente and the Pirates defeated our division-rival Baltimore Orioles, baseball permeated my very being. The slightest news—

the Dodgers trading us backup catcher Tom Haller—sent my heart pulsing. Haller had, after all, once hit 27 home runs for San Francisco and I could imagine him contributing more to our team, Billy Martin's team, a squad of fellows whose names spring forth to this day with not a bit of prodding: Bill Freehan, our perennial All-Star; powerful Norm Cash, the fun-loving Texan; scrappy Dick McAuliffe; Cuba-born Tony Taylor, who blessed himself with the sign of the cross before each at bat; gangly, bespectacled Eddie Brinkman, flawless in 72 straight games at shortstop; young Aurelio Rodriguez, whose name rolled like poetry; Al Kaline and Mickey Lolich and muscular, brooding, endearing Willie Horton; slick Mickey Stanley; grand-slam slugging Jim Northrup; Ike and Gates Brown, eternal part-timers; boyish Joe Coleman; Tom Timmerman, who in black-rimmed glasses looked more like a math teacher than a pitcher; and I could go on: Bill Slayback, Paul Jata, Joe Niekro, big Frank Howard, Fred Scherman, Chuck Seelbach. . . .

No doubt, you also can recall your favorite childhood team.

My father remembers his: Gehringer, Greenberg, Owen, Cochrane, Goslin, Fox, White, Walker, Bridges, Rogell. Dad was a teenager when they played together in the mid-1930s. Almost all of them have passed, but he talks of them yet and there's magic in his voice when he does.

You never forget those men, just as you never forget the year the sport became something more than a way to pass time. It remains as familiar as the faces on the ball cards. It comes back to you thirty years on when someone mentions a name—maybe Reichardt—and you think "Rick," and you wonder, do I know a Rick Reichardt? And suddenly, though you've not thought of him in decades, you realize he was a ball player, an outfielder with the Chicago White Sox who hit two home runs off the Tigers in one game. In 1972.

You may know that year for Nixon and McGovern and Watergate or for Archie Bunker or Mark Spitz or Moon Buggies or *The Poseidon Adventure* or the way Roberta Flack sang. Mostly I remember it for baseball—for Johnny Bench and Charlie Finley, for our playoff-bound Tigers, for Luis Tiant's jerky pitching motion, and, especially, for the Cooperstown wish that dominated my thoughts and words that summer—a wish that persisted longer than even Nolan Ryan's career.

That's how I like to remember 1972. In truth, there was much more to it. I see that now.

Not long ago I ran into an old ball-playing buddy, and after the courteous questions about family and jobs, our conversation curved toward baseball. Remembering how he loved the sport as a boy, I mentioned that I had been to the Hall of Fame.

"Damn," he said. He gave his eyes a long blink, snapped his head forward, and beamed like Tommy Lasorda. "That's great. I want to go there someday. What did it take? Nine or ten hours?"

"Twenty-nine years," I said.

He laughed. But it was the truth.

This book is about that journey. It's about a trip to Cooperstown in the August of one recent summer, a trip that lasted just two days but took nearly three decades to realize. My father, my brother, and I had been talking of going to Coopers-town since Willie Mays played at Candlestick Park, back before free agency when young stars yearned to reach the magical $100,000-a-year plateau, back when umpires wore chest protectors over their uniforms and American League pitchers batted for themselves and at least a few of our heroes stayed with one team their entire careers. A long time back, in other words. A time that fans my age see as a little more perfect in a baseball sense.

But everyday life—350 months' worth—intruded on my Cooperstown wish.

Finally, in the summer of 2001 after the publication of my last book, I received an invitation to speak at the Baseball Hall of Fame. Quicker than the snap of Henry Aaron's wrists, I accepted.

"When are you going?" my brother asked.

"You want to come?"

"Yeah, maybe."

"How about you, Dad?"

"Well, either way," he said, a response typical of my father. "Whatever works best for you." To a stranger it might have sounded like tepid interest. But my dad has always insisted on putting everyone else's desires first. He wanted to come; I knew that.

This book is also about a journey of a different kind, one for which I hadn't planned or dreamed, a journey that involves my relationship with my father and my brother, the two people most responsible for my love of the game.

At the time of the trip, Dad was eighty-one and my brother

Joey and I were in our forties, me just barely, him closer to fifty, both of us long married and with children of our own, his three out of high school, mine a bit younger. In the 1960s when Dad was our age, we took family vacations together, all of us, Mom and my sisters, too. But until the trip to Cooperstown we three guys had never ventured off separately, and given the nature of our lives it seemed unlikely we would find many other opportunities.

I was thrilled to have my brother join me but I was especially relieved that Dad would be with us. He's the glue. Though my brother and I have always gotten along and though we see each other frequently at family gatherings and have rarely had cause to fight, we are separated by seven years. And I think because of those years we have never been exceptionally close.

We didn't stand up at each other's weddings, never talked about girlfriends the way brothers of similar ages might, never hung out together, never even contemplated forming a family musical group, like the Cowsills.

Aside from baseball and family, I wasn't sure what we had in common. We differ politically, religiously, professionally, socially, and in numerous other ways. I wondered whether our trip, though brief, might feel strained. I certainly never expected it would change us. But it has.

Every true baseball fan harbors dreams of visiting Cooperstown. But why? What compels us to travel to an out-of-the-way village in upstate New York? Why do hundreds of thousands of us undertake the same trip each year? Why do movies like *A League of Their Own* and novels by writers as diverse as W. P. Kinsella and Richard Ford put their characters on the road to Cooperstown?

Those who have never felt the sweet pull of baseball's gravity struggle to understand its hold on us. It perplexes some. It causes others to shake their heads knowingly, smirking lovingly as if we've been walking with toilet paper on our heels again, as if we're behaving strangely because the dentist's laughing gas has yet to wear off or because the hypnotist has us barking like dogs. They act as if we're oblivious to a harmless affliction that has altered our personalities.

But we're the fortunate ones.

Baseball's appeal isn't complicated or confusing. It's about the beauty of a game; it's about heroes and family and friends; it's about being part of something larger than yourself, about belonging; it's about tradition—receiving it and passing it; and it's about holding on to a bit of your childhood.

Doesn't it start there for most of us, in childhood?

That's where this story begins.

1. Spring 1972: Cobb's Birthday

My father, Joseph Stankiewicz, was born in 1920, the same year Carl Mays accidentally killed Cleveland infielder Ray Chapman by beaning him with a fastball. My mother, Betty Muse, arrived two seasons later, days after Wally Pipp and teammate Babe Ruth went at it in the dugout. But please don't read into those associations. There is no correlation. Mom was feisty, not violent, and Dad, though stubborn, certainly would have relinquished the inside of the plate rather than take a ball to the head.

The Chapman and Pipp incidents say nothing about my parents, but they say everything about me and how I pictured the world as a boy: as spinning on an axis of baseball. Everywhere I looked, I found parallels to my life and the game. I remembered dates by placing them on baseball's timeline; I remembered people by connections I conjured between them and the men who wore the uniforms.

My parents met during World War II, when Dad was stationed in St. Joseph, Missouri, close to Mom's home, and at a time when Ted Williams, who had enlisted in the Navy, was giving baseball fans something more to remember him by: a Triple Crown performance. Long before Mom caught Dad's eye in a soldiers' hangout near Rosecrans Field, Dad was hitching rides to town with her stepfather, a carpenter who built barracks. He was a strapping, sturdy farmer, and when I see pictures of Cy Young I think of him. Mom's mother, who smiled tight-lipped like Ty Cobb, was a pioneer woman who wore dungarees and ball caps and could shoot the head off a rattler from twenty feet.

Mom and Dad came from different, Depression-era worlds, neither well-to-do. Mom and her three sisters (a brother died young) lived in small towns and on farms in Missouri, Nebraska, and Kansas, their American roots nine generations deep. Dad grew up in an industrial city, Detroit, born to Polish immigrants. His mother raised him and his nine siblings to be good Catholics. His father raised him to love baseball.

They married in 1944 and moved from Missouri about the time Mickey Mantle was making news in the minors at Joplin, where, depending on whose stories you believe, he may or may not have gotten drunk with Uncle Grubby. My parents settled in the Detroit area to raise their children, each separated by four to seven years: first came Jan, who followed Jackie Robinson into the spotlight; then Joey, a rookie with Hank Aaron; next, me; and finally Colleen, a bigger 1965 surprise than Zoilo Versalles.

I was born in 1960, the year Bill Mazeroski won the World Series for Pittsburgh. But it's the date, not the year, that's important. I was born on December 17, and, sure, by itself maybe it means nothing. But when you're a boy who lives for baseball and you're studying the crisp-tissue pages of *The Baseball Encyclopedia* and you stumble upon the fact that Ty Cobb was born on December 18 and then discover that Al Kaline was born on December 19, well, you begin to see something at work. It's destiny, not mere coincidence, that aligns your birthday with those of the two greatest Tigers.

We arrived on Shawn Drive before Colleen was born. It was our second home. The neighborhood had sprouted from a cornfield in the three-year-old city of Warren. By the end of Sandy Koufax's career, it stretched for three-quarters of a Michigan mile: hundreds of nearly identical ranch homes on sixty-foot lots and slow-speed streets, with smooth, chalk-gray sidewalks and scrawny, curb-side saplings, with yards fenced and garages attached and young white families like ours inside, moving up in the world as we moved out from the city.

Few secrets survived on Shawn Drive. We kids ensured that, several dozen of us in a space no bigger than Fenway's outfield. The Knudsens—their living room decorated with china teacups and a portrait of Queen Elizabeth II—had come from Canada with four sons. All played hockey and soccer, some well enough to attract scouts. The Elliots had three children. The girl with long blond hair danced on *American Bandstand* and, while her parents worked, occasionally allowed her hippie friends to skinny-dip in the pool behind their house. (You would have watched, too.) The Metts boys lived down the street near the

Pellegrinos, who knew sign language because their father was deaf, and across from Tom Norkiewicz, a red-haired boy whose dad was a policeman—"the fuzz," as my brother might have said. Next door were the Newmans, featuring little Jimmy, who sometimes shocked the Burchette sisters by showing them what made boys different. There were also the Hellickers, Ostrowskis, Lewandowskis, and the second nicest man on the block, Mr. Woitha. When Johnny Woitha, his oldest teenage son, went for surgery, the kids from Shawn Drive gathered along the sidewalk to send him off with well wishes. Johnny smiled and waved from the car, and that's the last picture we have of him. He died in the hospital. Despite his anguish, Mr. Woitha always managed a hearty grin for us children who passed his house as he mowed the lawn.

My best friend, Jeff Mancini, lived across the street. He was months younger and a grade lower, the oldest of four boys who came one right after another. Jeff looked like his dark-haired, Italian dad, who raced cars professionally. You could often find Mr. Mancini—or hear him—in his garage working on a candy apple–red Dodge that he drove to victory at the drag nationals. On our street he was the closest we had to a celebrity.

Jeff and I shared a devotion to baseball. In the spring of 1972, our collective lives centered on the sport. If we weren't practicing with the St. Malachy Tigers, we were playing Strikeout with a rubber ball against a wall or hitting each other grounders on the school's brick-hard field or alternating as pitcher and catcher against an army of invisible power hitters in the last of the ninth with the game on the line and Boog Powell at the plate and then Richie Allen and George Scott and Harmon Killebrew and even Mike Epstein. Many of our baseball adventures took place at Robert Frost Elementary, which seemed fitting in that Robert Frost loved the sport. "I never feel more at home in America than at a ball game," the poet said.

Some of my best baseball memories include Jeff.

Often, he and I would be sorting cards—by team, not number—wondering how it was possible to get so many of Dalton Jones, or exploring the rivalries of the day, feigning impartiality but always deciding in favor of our Tigers. Yeah, we would agree, Mickey Lolich pitches way better than Vida Blue. For sure, Bill Freehan will be the All-Star catcher again. Ray Fosse and Thurman Munson don't have a prayer, and Elrod Hendricks and Andy Etchebarren, well, they're both so bad that Earl Weaver won't let none of them catch full-time. And speaking of Weaver, Billy Martin could take him in a fight. And no way would we trade Kaline for Clemente or Willie Horton for Reggie Smith or Aurelio Rodriguez for Ken McMullen. We matched the Tigers against the Baltimore Orioles, who had won the division title the three years prior, 1969–71, and had played in the past two World Series. They were the enemies: Brooks, Boog, Belanger, Blair, and Buford, and a pitching staff with four twenty-game winners. But no matter who they had—and they no longer had Frank Robinson, incidentally—by our calculations they were no competition for Billy Martin's team.

Before coming to Detroit, Martin had managed only one year, taking the Minnesota Twins to first place and into the playoffs against Weaver's Orioles. He succeeded Mayo Smith, who had brought us a world championship but couldn't tame wild Denny McLain. Billy Martin resurrected the Tigers in 1971—or did they resurrect him?—and vowed to oust Weaver from first place in the campaign about to begin.

"Billy Martin should be an evangelist," said Weaver. "He's got you guys believing he's got the best team again. He's done that now every year he's been in the league. To hear him talk in 1969, we had no business even showing up for the playoffs. Then we had his Twins down two games to none and he announced he had us right where he wanted us."

Brash, feisty, and often angry, Billy Martin fit the times and our region. He had a testosterone-fueled edge that mirrored the acrimony over the Vietnam War, cross-district busing, race, and "women's liberation."

Dad disliked Martin. He reminded him of every mean, blowhard drunk he had ever known. "It's always somebody else's fault with him," he said.

Martin's emotions swung to extremes, one year feuding with Willie Horton and the next proclaiming him the soul of the team. Cruelty burnt in his eyes. In contrast, my dad rarely raised his voice—and never his fists. But such subtleties are lost on the young.

To a boy, there was something appealing about Billy Martin. He was like one of the tough kids at school with whom you formed a fragile alliance. You liked him mostly because he was on your side. Billy Martin had bluster and bravado, and he had promised victory. And not much was more important than that.

On a morning in spring while writing letters to Willie Stargell and Dock Ellis—we decorated the envelopes in yellow and black to ensure they would be plucked from the mail pile—Jeff Mancini and I began talking about the inevitable, about the day we would make it to the majors. At forty I see that dream through a mist of nostalgia. But it looked different then. It looked as solid as Johnny Bench. We talked about it with the same certainty we talked about everything. Jeff would be shortstop; I would be center fielder. Eddie Brinkman and Mickey Stanley would be old, in their late thirties, and retired, and we'd be out of high school and ready to play.

"And let's be roommates, okay?"

"Yeah, like Gale Sayers and Brian Piccolo."

"Except for the dying part."

"And we can share a house."

"Yeah, with three bedrooms. One for me, one for you, and one for all our trophies."

"And a big basement with paneling and white-shag carpeting and a pool table and a bar."

"And a huge TV."

"A colored TV."

"I know how to make hot dogs and chili."

Jeff adjusted his cap.

"And we can get pizza a lot because we'll be making a lot of money."

"Yeah, about thirty thousand dollars."

"Heck, more than that."

"And we'll play twenty years."

"No, twenty-four. Like Ty Cobb."

"And retire at the same time."

"Then when we both get married, we'll get houses next to each other."

"Our kids will be best friends, too."

"And we'll go into the Hall of Fame together."

We mapped our futures in ten minutes' time, never doubting that baseball would always be the focal point of our lives, certain that we would be best friends forever, believing that it would end where all baseball dreams end, at the Hall of Fame in Cooperstown, New York.

The *Sporting News* greeted the scheduled start of the season with an issue featuring Roberto Clemente on the cover. "Pirates' Mister Big," it said. Inside was a locker-room photo of the star holding a sign with the number 3,000 on it, alluding to the hitting mark he hoped to reach. It preceded a story about another National League legend, Hank Aaron, who needed 76 home runs to top Babe Ruth. "If I can remain healthy I'm confident I can break the record," Aaron said. "If I don't I guess it's not too bad being runner-up to the Babe."

Deeper in the publication, other articles detailed a brewing dispute that threatened to bring baseball's first full-scale players' strike. Publisher C. C. Johnson Spink came down firmly on the owners' side, questioning the logic of pensions for players. "Baseball is not a career in the true sense of the word," he wrote. "Instead, it is just an interlude—and a rewarding one—before the player embarks on what should be his real profession or occupation."

The players struck that spring, ending training camp abruptly, an action that Billy Martin took personally. He stormed through the locker room calling his players "pot-lickers." "They've pulled my whole team out from under me," Martin told reporters. "Somebody doesn't want me to win." I couldn't figure out who that somebody might be. The newspapers carried a photo of the players' attorney, Marvin Miller, looking as evil as Satan in slicked-back hair, with Reggie Jackson at his side in a wide-lapelled coat and defiant mustache. Maybe it was them. Maybe Reggie didn't want us to win.

The strike spanned thirteen days. When the season finally opened, it was a cold, damp Saturday and the Boston Red Sox were in town. Dad, who had worked that morning at the tank command (he was a government photographer), melted into the afghan-covered couch in front of the console. I sat on the floor beside him, the sliding back door partially open. The two of us spent many Saturday afternoons together watching the local broadcast or the Game of the Week with Joe Garagiola. A couple years earlier and my brother Joey might have been with us.

There comes a time, though, when your older brother isn't around much, when his existence overlaps yours only along the edges. He reaches eighteen and though he may be in high school, he lives a life that flourishes beyond the walls of home. It's his senior year, and he has a job at the meat shop, a romance with the butcher's daughter, and adventures with longhair friends who take him away most evenings. You see little of him, and you notice because it used to be different. Before the girlfriend and the car, before he talked so much about The War, before he got an eight-track and began listening to music your parents had never heard, you could tag along as he went trick-or-treating on Halloween or hide out with him in his snow fort while it incurred a friendly assault or cling to the side of the swimming pool while he dunked his pals. If you lost your grip and slipped into water above your eyes, he would retrieve you and return you to the safe perimeter. If it happened too often, he would thump your head and order you out of the pool. For a long while it was that way with us.

But by 1972 Joey had lost interest in the game. He said there were more important things. By that he meant Vietnam and his girlfriend and George McGovern and the draft and Sly and the Family Stone and his artwork—all-white, life-size papier-mâché sculptures of anonymous people, silk screens of the Zig Zag man, eight-foot canvases of vibrant blue-and-orange toilets.

Anymore, Dad and I watched the games without him.

With my father a broad landscape of baseball lay before us. He had decades of stories that I mined endlessly. He painted an enchanting picture of his younger days and of Ty Tyson's radio broadcasts in the 1930s and of neighborhood ball games and of streetcar rides to Navin Field, where the Tigers played. It sounded like such an adventure that I often wished I had grown up in that time. He pulled names from the '30s and '40s as if listing the guys in his Air Corps outfit. For every one of my Manny Sanguillens, he had a Mickey Cochrane, a Gabby Hartnett, and a Yogi Berra. For every Jim Palmer, a Bob Feller; for every Pete Rose, a Pie Traynor. It was impossible for us to watch a game without mentioning the Hall of Fame because so many of the men he had admired as a boy—Charlie Gehringer, Hank Greenberg, Cochrane, Goslin—had been inducted by 1972.

Gehringer was his favorite, an example of quiet greatness, the Al Kaline of his day. When Dad talked of Gehringer, two stories surfaced. First, that Gehringer never swung at the first pitch. He was patient, Dad said, and we both knew good things came to those who waited. Second, that after his father died, Charlie took care of his mother, bought her a home, and refused to marry until she had passed. I suspected Dad had a reason for telling me of Charlie's devotion over and over again and that it probably had something to do with my mother's illness.

Charlie Gehringer—there was a man worth admiring.

Mickey Lolich, one of my favorites, pitched our 1972 opener. He was coming off a sterling season for which he would have received the Cy Young Award had it not been for flashy, young, unappreciative Vida Blue.

In the first inning Lolich fell into trouble, surrendering four singles. But the Red Sox managed only one run.

"George Kell played for them," Dad said, nodding at the screen as the Boston players took their positions. Kell broadcast Detroit games, his voice imbued with a gentle Arkansas drawl. He had been a Tiger in the '40s before heading to Boston.

"Was he any good?"

"Yeah, very good. A third baseman. He was an All-Star. Played with Hoot Evers and Vic Wertz. We should never have traded him."

"Who'd we get?"

"Pesky—Johnny Pesky—and Walt Dropo. They didn't amount to much. Pesky was over the hill."

Dad looked at his open-faced cheese sandwich, topped with a puddle of ketchup, and he angled a corner into his mouth, careful not to drip on his work shirt, which was tight at the belly and blotched by darkroom chemicals. He washed it down with a swig of pickle juice. I cringed.

Dad had an unusual appetite. He ate mustard-and-onion sandwiches. He made meatball soup. He liked beet juice on mashed potatoes. He scrambled eggs with diced hot dogs. He poured vinegar on bologna, and he doused everything with ketchup. But it was the pickle juice that got to me.

"Is George Kell in the Hall of Fame?"

I had never seen pictures of the Hall of Fame, had never talked to anyone who had been there. It had the same mythical quality as the North Pole, and it seemed about as far away. But announcers often mentioned it and so did newspaper writers, and *Baseball Digest*—with its one-color covers and black-and-white photos—carried stories about players who had been overlooked, like Ralph Kiner, Gil Hodges, and Johnny Mize. It was clear that for a ball player nothing topped Cooperstown. Only the best of the best made it. It was baseball heaven.

"Gehringer and Greenberg are in there." Dad said their names as if they were a Vaudeville act, the Amazing Gehringer & Greenberg.

"Kaline will get in, don't you think?"

"Oh, yeah. He'll get there someday."

"What about Mickey Lolich?"

"Well, maybe."

He often substituted "maybe" for "no."

"Why not?" I asked, getting defensive on Mickey's behalf.

"He's a good ball player," Dad said, "but he's got to win more games. Bob Feller won twenty games a lot of times. Lolich did it once. But, who knows, maybe he'll get there."

His weak endorsement sounded like a betrayal of Mickey Lolich, who had stepped from Denny McLain's shadow to win three games in the 1968 World Series and who had led the league in victories three years later.

I liked Lolich. He rode motorcycles and looked like the kind of guy who might live on our street. Al Kaline didn't. Kaline was an untouchable in the hero caste system. If they had been actors, Kaline would have been Jimmy Stewart and Lolich would have been Ernest Borgnine. Kaline had a presence that proclaimed him too good for our neighborhood, too athletic, too upright, too rich. Not that we wouldn't have loved for him to live among us. It's just that we knew he never would. But imperfect Mickey Lolich, with his belly, would have fit right in, changing his car oil in the driveway, gulping a can of Altes beer on the porch, dangerously reigniting the charcoal-grill fire by squirting starter fluid into the fading flames.

Lolich cruised through the Boston lineup—Tommy Harper, Aparicio, Yastrzemski, Reggie Smith, Petrocelli. Dad finished his pickle juice, and I sipped my Towne Club orange-pineapple soda.

"Me and Jeff are gonna be in the Hall of Fame someday," I announced.

"Well, I don't doubt it for a minute," he said.

His words felt like feathers and I let them float there for a few pitches and then, trying to profit from the pleasant mood, asked in a voice as soft as marshmallows, "Can we go to the Hall of Fame?"

Dad turned from the television and paused as if that thought had never occurred to him.

"Yeah, maybe someday," he said.

"Can we go this summer?"

"We'll have to see."

"But maybe?"

"I don't know."

"But maybe?"

He tilted his head and sighed. "You sure have a one-track mind."

"But maybe?"

"We'll see."

"Please maybe can we go this year?"

If he had just refused, he would have spared both of us a whole lot of heartache. For he must have known at that moment that the trip wouldn't happen, that it couldn't with Mom being sick and another of her brain surgeries threatening our horizon.

But he exhaled hard and said, "Maybe." Which in this context I took to mean "Yes."

For a long time, I didn't understand why he hadn't just said no that afternoon. I didn't understand that until I was his age with children of my own.

2. Twenty-Nine Years Later

In the movie A League of Their Own, *members of the Rockford Peaches women's baseball team gather in Cooperstown for a reunion.*
"Baseball's Hall of Fame," says player Marla Hooch, approaching the shrine.
"I'm shaking," adds Shirl Baker.

It's an early Thursday morning in August 2001, an hour before sunrise, and we're finally leaving for Cooperstown. It's just Dad, Joey, and me, and we're embarking on our first overnight trip together.

I can't help but wonder, as I do more and more, where the time has gone. Johnny Bench is in his fifties, and Al Kaline has been retired twenty-seven years—more years than he played. Mantle is dead; DiMaggio, too. Ruth's record fell long ago when I was thirteen; Cobb's record, eleven years later; and Gehrig's, a decade after that. And if that sounds a bit too heavy and depressing, if the tone strikes as maudlin or melancholy, I do apologize. I don't mean it that way. It's just a fact. Almost three decades have passed since 1972. Dad is eighty-one now, not fifty-two. He remains sharp-minded, healthy, and independent, though hampered by lousy hearing. Joey is forty-seven, not eighteen, and I'm forty, not eleven. People recognize us as brothers. They say there is a resemblance, which troubles me. (If you saw him, you would understand.)

Look, the bottom line is this: I've waited a long time to go to Cooperstown. Longer than Satchel Paige. But regardless of how many years have passed, I feel like a boy today, a boy with a driver's license, a Montana minivan, and a receding Yogi Berra hairline.

I still call my brother Joey and he still calls me Tommy, and that probably says something about our relationship, though what I'm not exactly sure.

I know the words sound infantile; they feel that way when I write them. But it would be false for me to call him the sterile word by which the rest of the world knows him: Joe. His co-workers, his neighbors, the receptionist at the dentist's office— they call him that. When he introduces himself, he says he's Joe. When he signs his name, he writes Joe. But he's always been Joey to me and I've always been Tommy to him.

For a time in high school we tried to escape those names. When you're heading into adulthood, you don't want your brother pulling you back to fourth grade. I don't mind anymore. It's nice to be drawn back there occasionally.

Forty-five years from now in the year 2046, after I've won three gold medals in the Senior Olympics, I'll phone my brother to share the news. By then he'll be in a convalescent home pondering cryogenics. He'll be much older and more senile and no longer able to resist the urge to wear women's undergarments. But I'll still be calling him Joey, and he'll be gumming out my name—Tommy—provided he remembers it.

And that's another thing about us. We tease each other a lot.

Someone once told me that such ribbing substitutes for intimacy. We are brothers, after all.

Dad, Joey, and I live in southeast Michigan, north of Detroit, roughly at the base of the thumb in our mitten-shaped state, between the Great Lakes of Huron and Erie. Most Americans know Canada as "Our Neighbor to the North," but where we live the country lies immediately east and even south. In some spots it is less than a half-mile across the water. If you're heading to New York from my house, you can cut an hour or two off the drive by going through Ontario.

It's dark when we cross the St. Clair River at the Port Huron–Sarnia border. Lines of streetlights speckle the neighborhoods below. In the distance car beams slide across the inky landscape. The shoreline glows with industry, the shadowy smoke from stacks escaping under cover, floating straight up into the predawn sky. The blue, Christmasy outline of the double-span bridge glistens on the river far down, and the view looks magical, like the scene in *Peter Pan* before they fly out the window into their adventure. (We won't take that analogy any further.)

WELCOME TO CANADA—THE WORLD NEXT DOOR, says the sign.

"Citizenship?" asks the guard at the gate.

"U.S."

She looks at Joey and me in the front seat and through the minivan's tinted side window at Dad in the back.

"Anyone else in the vehicle? . . . Do you have any firearms, drugs, or alcohol? . . . How long will you be in Canada? . . . Purpose of your trip?"

And that is a good question: What is the purpose of our trip?

It seems simple enough: to have a good time together at the Hall of Fame. But is that all? Isn't there something more that each of us wants from this trip? To celebrate baseball? To reclaim our childhoods? To connect with our heroes? To strengthen our bond to those with whom we've shared the sport? That must be part of it for everyone who makes the journey. But I suspect there are more personal reasons as well, and that maybe we won't figure them out until we get there, if at all.

For my dad I think it's about being with us, his two sons. Not that we're such marvelous company, but he seems to enjoy us (and we do enjoy him).

Earlier this summer while in Dayton, Ohio, promoting my last book, a crusty former sportswriter in his late seventies told me how his adult son had come to town on business and invited him to a ball game at Cinergy Field in Cincinnati. Decades earlier the father and son had shared games there when it was Riverfront Stadium and Sparky Anderson was a young manager. "My son has given me a lot of things," the man said. "But that was the best gift, going to the ballpark with him. I don't think he knows how much it meant."

Purpose of our trip?

Should I say something intriguing? Something mysterious? Should I be coy? Should I explain that we're pursuing an old dream, fulfilling a wish that refused to die? She would understand. We all have dreams born in childhood. Sometimes they slip into the recesses of our memories with a million other forgotten facts: phone numbers, names, batting averages. Other times they linger for ten, twenty, almost thirty years, whispering in the night, calling out in wistful moments, sweetly reminding of unfinished business.

"Purpose of your trip?" the border guard asks.

"We're going to Cooperstown, New York. The Baseball Hall of Fame."

"Enjoy yourselves," she says.

She waves us through the gate, and we are finally on our way.

3. Rocky's Muscles

"There is not much that I can say except that I feel very much honored and very happy to be here this day, one of baseball's most eventful days."

—Ty Cobb in Cooperstown for the first induction

Highway 402 leads out of Sarnia, Ontario. It cuts through flat farmland and passes towns with Anglo names like Warwick, Watford, Cairngorm, Strathroy, and Lambeth. You get a sense quickly that you've arrived in another country: crown emblems on highway signs, speed limits set in kilometers, radio stations that play Gino Vannelli (you know, 1978, ". . . the wheels of life are turning so much faster now, the restless hands of time pass me by . . .").

But Dad senses it in something else.

"They sure have a lot of them Tim Hortons restaurants," he says.

Almost every exit along 402 will put you within a short drive of a Tim Hortons, a Dunkin' Donuts kind of place with sandwiches and soup. There are 1,900 of them in Canada, and they're more prevalent than McDonald's. And they're all named for one hockey player, which could only happen here, where hockey reigns as the national pastime.

Tim Horton spent almost twenty years in the NHL. "Mostly with Toronto," says Dad. His first doughnut shop opened in the mid-1960s when he was an All-Star defenseman. Some fans think he invented the slap shot; others, the apple fritter. By February 1974 Horton had become a Sabre. That month while speeding back to Buffalo, he crashed his Pantera sports car along the QEW, Queen Elizabeth Way, and died. His business partner bought out his interest and in time expanded extensively, keeping the name and surviving a legal battle in the 1990s with the player's widow.

We stop at a Tim Hortons shortly after crossing the U.S.–Canada border. A hint of daylight slits the cloudy, darkened sky along the horizon. Dad tugs on the minivan's side door, which resists his efforts.

"It's electric," I say.

He watches the door glide back. An ornery man might view it as an insult or wonder why the hell you need an automatic door when you can open it more quickly yourself. But Dad's not ornery, never has been, and he has grown even kinder with age.

We breeze through Tim's place, leaving with two coffees and a bag of bagels slathered in cream cheese.

"Dad, don't you want something to drink?" Joey asks in the cool of the parking lot. "They have other stuff besides coffee. You want a Coke or some juice or water?"

"No, no. I'm fine."

"You sure?"

"I'm fine."

My brother glances at me.

"Nothing?" I ask.

"Nothing," Dad says, and then he changes the subject. "Didn't Mickey Lolich used to own a doughnut shop?"

In 1983, weeks out of college, I started a small magazine with friends. It would soon flop, but the third issue—the final one— featured an interview with Lolich at his suburban doughnut shop. He had retired from baseball years earlier, finishing his career with San Diego, where he won the last of his 217 victories.

Given the paunch that Lolich carried throughout his career, fans saw his leap into the baked-sweets business as natural. He, however, felt destined to work with motorcycles. He had been riding them since his earliest days in Oregon.

Dressed in baker's white, Lolich played the cordial host, posing for photos, sharing his insights, and griping about Vida Blue winning the 1971 Cy Young Award.

"Most fans remember that I won three games in the World Series," he said. "I've won three games in ten days many times in my career. They just weren't on national television. Winning three games in the World Series could be a fluke. But 1971—it took a whole season. Nobody ever remembers 1971."

"Well, I remember it," I interjected, thinking it might impress him. "You had an amazing season."

But he didn't acknowledge my words, just kept talking as if no one remembered.

Lolich recited the stats like a jilted husband recounting all he had contributed to a failed marriage: 25 wins, 376 innings, 29 complete games, 45 games started, 308 strikeouts. And still she left me, it meant nothing in the end, all the years I gave her. . . . "The only category I lost that year was earned run average—and they gave Vida Blue the Cy Young Award."

Lolich sprinkled cinnamon and sugar on a sheet of dough, rolled it into a loaf, and sliced it with a pastry knife—with his right hand.

"No, you're left-handed," I wanted to tell him. "I saw you pitch. You're definitely left-handed."

He noticed my perplexed look.

"I'm right-handed," he said.

When Lolich was two, he explained, a motorcycle fell on his right shoulder and injured it. He learned to throw a baseball with his left arm. "My career was an accident."

When the publication containing the Lolich article came out, Dad took a couple hundred copies and distributed them door-to-door on his lunch hour. So he knows the story. But in the backseat of the minivan he acts as if it is as fresh as his Tim Hortons bagel.

"That was quite an accident," Dad says.

"You sure you don't want something to drink?"

"No. I'm fine."

Between Sarnia and Toronto, my brother notices an exit sign for the Canadian Baseball Hall of Fame. "Who'd be in there?" he wonders.

"Fergie Jenkinson," Dad says.

He means Ferguson Jenkins. Dad mispronounces words because of his poor hearing. He lives near County Line Road but calls it Country Lane Road. He shops at VG's Market but refers to it as VJ's. It's a harmless trait, unless you're getting directions.

I had stopped at the Canadian Hall of Fame last summer. It was closed. It's in a converted house that sits on a hill above a ball field in St. Marys, a town of historic stone buildings. My wife, Beth, and I were on our way back from Stratford, a nearby Shakespearean village where we see plays. St. Marys, like Cooperstown, hides in the countryside.

"Maybe you don't need to be Canadian to get inducted," Joey continues. "The Blue Jays and Expos have had some decent players."

We're both trying not to snicker at the idea of a Canadian Baseball Hall of Fame. It seems the polite thing to do. Still, it strikes us as funny.

"Yeah, well Andre Dawson, Tim Raines, Dave Steib—they played in Canada," I say.

"Jack Morris and Roger Clemens," he adds.

"Gary Carter played for the Expos."

"Joe Carter. Jesse Barfield."

"Now you're scraping."

"Didn't Phil Niekro pitch for the Blue Jays?"

"John Hiller grew up here."

"Is Larry Walker Canadian?"

"Dad, can you think of any ball players from Canada?"

I say it again, louder this time.

"Reno Bertoia?" he wonders.

Born in Italy and raised near Windsor (across the border

from Detroit), Bertoia signed with the Tigers in 1953 at eighteen. Dad was thirty-three, married with one daughter, and starting his career as a government photographer. His father, Theodore Stankiewicz, a Chrysler employee, liked to spend Sundays at Northwestern Field, where Bertoia played Class D ball. It was a different time, and stories of the local kid being scouted and signed by the local major-league team made headlines.

Longtime fans recognize Bertoia's name yet because of his status as a "bonus baby"—and probably because they feel he never fulfilled his potential. Bertoia flashed in late May 1957, challenging The Great Ted Williams—"The Great" was implied when Dad talked—for the league lead with a .375 batting average. But he never again approached that number. Playing close to home "I was always afraid of disappointing somebody," he said in retirement. He was so nervous that the Tigers gave him tranquilizers on game days. That worked for a while.

Bertoia spent an unremarkable five years, half of his career, as a part-time player with the Tigers. He skipped the minor leagues like another teenager, his more successful roommate, Al Kaline.

As adults we think most fondly of the players who found their way into our dreams before our voices changed, who sparked in us the kind of devotion that couldn't be shed by slumps or slights, whose stances we emulated and stats we memorized, whose faces we most hoped to see in our packs of Topps cards, behind the powdery flat sticks of gum and amid the team pictures and Series II checklists and the likenesses of other teams' journeyman players.

Among a certain age of fans, it would be sacrilegious to admit that you never worshipped Mickey Mantle or Willie Mays. I do place them among the pantheon of baseball gods with Ruth and Gehrig and DiMaggio and Aaron and a few others, but I never idolized them. Mantle finished his career in 1968 before being imprinted upon my memory, and Mays was an aging legend when I turned twelve. I remember him in the 1973 Series, misplaying a ball at age forty-two, his speed gone and his skills deteriorating, not the same man who in scratchy black-and-white footage snatched Vic Wertz's long drive at the Polo Grounds.

I can appreciate Mantle and Mays the same way I appreciate Joe DiMaggio, as historic figures, as legends. I admire their abilities. They were unquestionably among the best to play the game. But that's not the same as idolizing them, is it?

There is a hierarchy of heroes, and I see it this way: first, icons like Ruth and Aaron and Johnny Bench, guys who inspired kids all across the country; second, brilliant players who engendered tremendous loyalty from fans who followed their teams, unquestionable Hall of Famers like Kaline and Brooks Robinson and Yastrzemski and Robin Yount; third, regional stars—the Ron Santos and Luis Tiants—who got wide recognition but maybe not as much as they deserved; and fourth, those strictly local heroes who endeared themselves one way or another: Gates Brown in Detroit, Jim Gantner in Milwaukee, Tommy Agee in New York.

For my dad, Gee Walker would have been on that fourth level. A driven, aggressive ballplayer, sometimes reckless, he hit over .300 in five of his first seven seasons. After the 1937 campaign, when Walker averaged .335, manager Mickey Cochrane—

a hero himself for bringing a world championship to Detroit—traded the young outfielder. The move provoked an uproar among fans. Their protests drew national press. "He is a real screwball . . . but Detroit likes that type of player," the *World-Telegram* reported. Dad counted Walker among his favorites, though far beneath Charlie Gehringer.

My brother and I embraced some of the same idols: Kaline, Norm Cash. But he liked Denny McLain, I liked Lolich. He liked Mantle, I liked Bench. He bragged of Rocky Colavito, I never saw him.

On the road to Cooperstown, my brother recalls Colavito's muscle-flexing routine, how he put the bat behind his neck and across his shoulders and hooked his arms over the ends of it and twisted and turned. Joey rolls his head to each side, demonstrating a few of the moves, and in his gyrations a necklace works its way out from underneath his shirt. It glints in the sun.

It's a gold cross.

When did my brother begin wearing a gold cross? He's never worn one before, not for faith or fashion, not that I've known anyway. He wore a weighty, brass peace sign around his neck in the late '60s and a puka-bead necklace when Carter was president and perhaps a few modest gold chains later on. But never a gold cross.

On a certain level I know a lot about my brother. All of us—Dad, siblings, spouses, our children, some in-laws—get together regularly to celebrate birthdays and we see each other on holidays and sometimes just casually. I can tell you about my nieces and nephew, what colleges they go to, what they're studying, what interests them, where they work, what music they listen to. I can tell you about family vacations and the big moments in their lives. We share all that. I can also tell you everything about what my siblings were like in the early 1970s—or what I thought they were like. In fact, when I talk about my brother—you know, those conversations where you're introducing your family in absentia to a friend—I still begin, "My brother Joey used to be a radical."

That's how I frame descriptions of him. "My brother used to be a radical." I say it as if everything that has happened since then can't possibly compare to those glory days.

Other areas of my brother's life I know little about. I can't tell you, for example, where he works now or where he worked a year ago. I have a vague idea of what he does, something about designing machines that make parts for the auto industry, that he does it on a computer. I know that he became active in a church a year or two ago but not much more than that.

Every week or so I get an e-mail from Joey. There in the electronic mailbox, among the letters from friends and the poorly targeted advertisements trying to lure me with the promise that "men will notice your cleavage," will be a heartwarming story from my brother, one of those uplifting tales that makes the rounds on the Internet and always ends with a proclamation of faith. It's an act of persuasion, a not-so-subtle effort to convert, and if it came from someone else I might take offense or view it as an intrusion. But it's from my brother, who has only the best of motivations. Yet, it is unlike anything he would ever have sent before and just another reminder of how much we have changed and how different we have become.

As a boy, I wanted desperately to be like Joey; now, that may be what he wants for me, too.

I follow baseball partly because I followed my brother.

In the summer of 1968 on a dry, dusty morning, he and his pals ventured over to the ball field at the Frost school. Joey didn't want me along but I had begged and Mom had insisted and so there I was behind the green backstop, hoping my brother would let me play.

"You're too little. You'll get hurt," he said.

He was fourteen, I was seven, and the gap felt like an ocean. I liked racing Hot Wheels; he liked kissing girls. The distance made for an unequal relationship. It ensured that we didn't view each other as competition. But it also meant that he got all the power and privilege and responsibility and that I couldn't help but envy and idolize him. In return he protected me. That was the unspoken agreement.

Some of my worst injuries, in fact, have occurred in the presence of my brother.

There was the time he got a new bike. We were racing, me on foot, him on the sparkling three-speed with handlebar gears. He had given me a generous head start, and I had made it to the Knudsens' driveway first. But as he approached from behind, I tripped and flopped onto the sidewalk right in his path. Fate gave him a chance to be Dudley Do-Right and rescue the endangered stranger on the railroad tracks. Instead, he barreled over my head. His front tire scorched a tread mark above one eye, and his chain scuffed an oily track upon my skull that a doctor closed with stitches.

Then there was the mishap at the playground. Joey and his friends were hanging out and smoking while younger brothers and sisters climbed monkey bars and teetered on seesaws. A tenth grader was testing the limits of a horse swing intended for small children. He pumped hard, trying to rise above the top bar. His wooden horse raised up and kicked the front of my unsuspecting head, opening a river of blood as red as Vada Pinson's ball cap. More stitches.

"You're too little, Tommy," my brother said at the diamond. "You'll get hurt."

The backstop stood like a prison wall, segregating me from the frivolity on the field. Joey and his friends cheered and bragged and taunted and argued over who played better. Kaline or Mantle? McLain or Gibson? Cash or Killebrew? They swung and pounded balls into the outfield toward Masonic Avenue. They flew fast around the bases. They celebrated when they crossed the plate.

Occasionally, someone would pop a foul over the backstop and it would bound off the dirt and ricochet away from the action.

"Tommy, get the ball," my brother would yell.

I would hurl it toward him, giving it a big arc so it would clear the fence. I hoped he would notice the strength of my throwing arm. But he didn't.

They formed a club of sorts, Joey and his friends, and I ached to be among them, to be included in their fun, to partake in their sophisticated baseball escapades. I figured early on that to be part of my brother's pack I would have to get better at baseball and so I began learning about the sport and waiting for the day I would join them on the field. He kept me waiting and waiting.

Dad liked to pose us for pictures at home. There are shots of us in our Easter outfits standing in front of his Plymouth. There are photos of us looking up the chimney for Santa and of us in Halloween costumes—Joey in Army fatigues, me in a poofy, flowery clown outfit that I can only hope was Mom's doing.

But my favorite picture shows the two of us in our 1960s living room on a woven black-and-silver sofa with a blond stereo console off to one side against a paneled wall. It's a Polaroid, and Joey's ten, bony in a T-shirt, his wispy hair parted strongly on the left and highlighted by the flash from the bulb of Dad's camera. I'm wedged between Joey and the arm of the sofa, three years old, in pajamas and robe, my hands clasped in prayerful benevolence on my lap, my legs too short to touch the floor, my thick socks almost wriggled free from my feet. My brother has his arm draped over my shoulder, and I'm smiling like there's no better place to be.

Something about that photo reminds me of 1969, the year of Mom's first brain surgery.

Grandma Muse had come up from Kansas on a Greyhound bus and quickly taken over the running of the household, freeing my dad to concentrate on her daughter. Grandma wore glasses with thick rims the color of root beer and no-nonsense slacks and shirts she had sewn herself. A hair net kept her reddish curls flat against her head and partly covered a hearing aid that was connected to a battery pack the size of a transistor radio. The pack hung around her neck and hid beneath her shirt, protruding from her boyish chest. (I didn't realize then that its flatness was the result of breast cancer.) Grandma also read lips, gently mouthing the words as she spoke them. "She hears everything except what you want her to hear," Dad warned.

Grandma had survived a handful of heart attacks and heart failures, cancer, and a wandering husband, Ike, whom she divorced in the 1920s in favor of his younger brother Roy. After Roy died, she and Ike lived two doors apart for some fifteen years, never speaking a word to each other. It might have been the lengthiest silent treatment on Earth. People described Grandma as independent and stubborn, traits that everyone implied contributed to her longevity.

"She'll live to see Halley's Comet come again," my mom liked to say.

Grandma brought hard peppermint candies with her from Kansas, as well as an aura of intrigue. She was unlike anyone I knew in Warren, Michigan. She lived on a farm and thought nothing of grabbing a chicken by the neck, twisting off its head, and cooking the bird for dinner. On one of her visits, she startled my friends as we surrounded a garter snake slithering through the grass. She pushed us aside and swung a hoe into it, decapitating it on the first try. Grandma had relatives who rode with the Jesse James gang, and she had a sister who while crossing a railroad bridge got her foot stuck in the tracks and died with her husband when a train struck them as he tried to free her.

When Grandma smiled, she smiled with her lips clasped like Ty Cobb, both of their expressions indicating that they knew something you didn't. We boys could do no wrong with her, and she rewarded us with snowball-size clumps of popcorn that she formed with clear Karo syrup. And that is what I most remember: the food, her cooking.

On the weekend after Mom's surgery, Grandma was frying eggs sunny side–up in a cast-iron skillet. We called them dirty eggs because she cooked them in bacon fat and they ended up brown and flecked with bacon crumbs. The whole kitchen smelt of bacon, the air thick and greasy.

We were preparing to leave for the hospital to visit Mom.

"Can Jeff Mancini come?" I asked.

"No, Tommy." Dad said. "Not this time."

"Please."

"Nope. Sorry."

"Why not?"

"There's too much going on."

"But we'll be good."

"No."

I begged and he refused and I begged some more.

"No," he snapped.

"But that's not fair."

"Knock it off, Tommy," Joey snarled. He was sitting across the table in front of a wall that had been papered with a paint-by-number seascape mural.

"Please, Daddy."

"No! For the last time, no!"

"Then I'm running away," I said.

He ignored the threat, dragging his hash browns through his ketchup.

"You sure are a little pistol," Grandma said. She bent to hug me and whispered in her creaky voice, "Honey, yer momma's sick and yer daddy's got a lot on his mind. You got to behave."

I shuffled my chair away from the kitchen table and stomped to my bedroom, loudly searching for a suitcase and opening and closing drawers as I pretended to pack it, confident he would relent, that he would let Jeff come to the hospital with us, that he would change his mind when he gauged my determination and saw that his refusal meant I would be leaving home for good—at age eight. How would he explain that to Mom?

Dad kept his ruby wedding ring in his closet in his grandfather's humidor. I rummaged through the cedar box. It had white-glass panels inside and it smelt of cigars. Dad stored keepsakes in it: two-dollar bills, silver coins from the 1800s, a red-white-and-blue JOHN F. KENNEDY—OUR NEXT PRESIDENT pin, a couple of ticket stubs from Briggs Stadium, and several Indian arrowheads that Grandma had found on her farm. The ring no longer fit him. It did not fit me either, not even my thumb. But I admired it, the strong gold band, the round stone red as a Lite-Brite peg, and I put it in my pocket.

At the front door I repeated my threats, giving him one last chance—this is it, one last chance, I'm going, you'll never see me again, you'll be sorry, one last chance. I slammed the door and stood there for a moment with an empty suitcase, a ruby ring, and no idea where to go next.

Sometimes when you feel overwhelmed by what you can't control, you struggle desperately to make something or somebody do as you wish.

I hid on the side of the house, gripping the handle of a large wicker-colored suitcase that was half my size. I must have looked funny when Joey found me there, for he was trying not to laugh but failing at it, which got me whimpering and then crying and then sobbing. And in one of those rare moments of kindness that stays with you forever, my brother—the tough ball player with studious glasses and straight blond hair trimmed above the ears—stopped smirking, looked down at his shoes, and put his arm on my shoulder.

"It's okay, Tommy," he said, and he led me back into the house.

4. Toronto and Buffalo

Brooklyn Dodger Pee Wee Reese and his son, Mark, flew to Albany, New York, and drove a rental car to Cooperstown for the Hall of Fame induction ceremony one year. From the hotel, according to writer Roger Kahn, they spotted a helicopter delivering Joe DiMaggio to the village along the lake. "How come we always drive in and DiMaggio gets a helicopter?" the son asked. The elder Reese responded: "Because there are Hall of Famers and then there is Joe DiMaggio."

The bright morning sun streams through the windshield, reflecting off my brother's bald head and into my eyes. Joey keeps his shades clipped to his green "Legends of Baseball" T-shirt. It's rush hour and the traffic has thickened. As the kilometers roll away, an uncomfortable realization strikes. We haven't passed Brantford, and we haven't noticed any signs for Niagara Falls or Buffalo or Fort Erie.

"Did you see Wayne Gretzky Parkway?" I ask.

"Was I supposed to be looking for it? I thought you knew the way."

"I do but you've been talking so much. What was the last town you saw?"

He can't remember.

Dad lets us sort out the mess, assuming we will get him to Cooperstown without his input.

"There's a sign for Milton."

Joey studies the map. He can't locate Milton.

We missed the turnoff for Highway 403 sixty miles back—or was that sixty kilometers? It takes another ten miles on side streets before I stop at a gas station for directions. We are in Toronto, and by the time we get back on the right path we will have squandered an hour or more.

Joey hasn't been to Toronto since his honeymoon. He married his seventh-grade girlfriend, Connie, in August 1973 as Tiger management tired of Billy Martin. The team, stuck in third place behind Baltimore and Boston, fired Martin that September after he was suspended for encouraging pitchers to throw spitballs. "I do things that make some people mad," he said. "But they don't stop to think that I may be right and they may be wrong."

At the wedding Joey wore a blue tuxedo with a whopping velvet bow tie. His hair hung to his shoulders in wisps, his long sideburns bushy.

I've visited Toronto several times, usually on purpose, and the city always gets me thinking about my brother. Sometimes it's because of the honeymoon. When I was twelve, he gave me a souvenir from that trip, a pink-and-gray two-dollar bill with a young Queen Elizabeth II on the front and with words in French and English. The bill is dated "Ottawa 1954," the year my brother was born. I carry it in my wallet to this day.

There is another reason as well: Vietnam.

If you grew up in the '60s and early '70s, you couldn't escape Vietnam. It touched your life in ways big and small. Sometimes it was just there in the background, like a droning refrigerator. Other times it flashed like a fire on your living room floor.

My sister Janis dated soldiers, and it was common to see men in uniform around our house. But they usually ended up overseas and out of our lives. One of them shipped off the winter after our Tigers won the World Series. I remember my sister crying, the sharp dark lines under her brown eyes softening and then blurring. When she wiped them, the mascara spread across her cheekbones. She looked like Brooks Robinson on game day, a swath of black on each side of his nose.

Even baseball wasn't immune. Though Vietnam did not touch it in the powerful, patriotic way that World War II did, the war did impact the game. Some players, like Johnny Bench, served in the reserves, and others, like Norm Cash, commented on the turmoil of the times. "I couldn't handle the younger generation, what with their protests and burning of buildings and stuff about the Vietnam War," he said. "I was brought up that if your country is at war, you ought to fight in it." The conflict—overseas and at home—sapped baseball of some of its romanticism. Per-game attendance dropped, and Hollywood stopped making movies about the national pastime. And was it mere coincidence that Curt Flood challenged baseball's reserve clause and sat out a season, putting us on the road to free agency, as war protests reached their zenith?

My brother became involved in the antiwar effort a year after helicopter pilot Michael O'Connor, the brother of his best friend Jim, was shot down by the Viet Cong. Michael was listed as missing in action, and Joey and his friends wore bracelets engraved with his name. Seasons later, in 1972, my brother received a low-number notice from the draft board. It came in a simple white envelope with the words SELECTIVE SERVICE in blue capital letters along the upper left edge. It marked the official confirmation that he might be called to serve, and it triggered a crusade by Mom to get Joey declared a conscientious objector. The backup plan involved going to Toronto.

Humor fuels our relationship. We tease each other about our foibles, our eating habits, and our looks (which, admittedly, borders on cruel given his huge, misshapen forehead). But I don't joke about Vietnam. He has regrets. I don't agree with him, but I understand.

Somewhere after Toronto, we're filled with wonder and a sense of discovery.

First, we hit Ontario wine country. Who would have guessed there was one?

Second, we notice an exit near Niagara Falls for Sodom Road. How'd you like that for your address?

Next, we spot a long-necked winged creature in a swampy area.

"Is that a crane?"

"Maybe a heron?"

"A loon?"

"Eddie Brinkman?"

Then we pass a sign for the Tobacco Heritage and History Museum.

"You think anybody makes pilgrimages to that place?"

"I doubt it," my brother says. "Why? Are we on a pilgrimage?"

There's no doubt when you cross Peace Bridge that you're leaving one country for another. You go from the royal Queen

Elizabeth Way to a city named for a symbol of the American frontier, the buffalo.

It's not yet noon when I hand my brother the atlas and say, "If we take I-190 to 198 to 33 to I-90, we should be able to cut off a few miles and make up some of the time you lost us in Toronto."

"You're pathetic," he says.

It looks easy on the map so we ignore the arrows pointing toward Albany and set out on our shortcut. Dad notices Dunn Tire Park, home of the Triple-A Buffalo Bisons, as we pass. It's a gorgeous minor-league park, and you can see its diamond from the freeway.

"I think this is right," Joey says. He directs us off the highway, and we end up on a nearly deserted road that runs beside industrial plants. It's the kind of place you avoid after dark.

"You sure this is right?"

He shrugs and distorts his goofy face.

Eventually we find a street that appears on the map and take it toward the downtown, a surprisingly charming place. We arrive in the restaurant district.

"You in a hurry for lunch, Dad?"

"I'm never in a hurry," he says chuckling.

There was a time he went nonstop. If he wasn't working at the tank arsenal, he was mowing the grass. Or framing Mom's paintings. Or rushing off to the hospital. Or changing the oil. Or shopping for groceries. He used to have high blood pressure but no more. He retired seventeen years ago, forced out when privatization eliminated his photography job. His new employer wanted him to work on computers. He did for a while. Then on a single day, they gave him Employee of the Month honors—and a pink slip.

In Buffalo we spot freeway signs in the distance and follow them to the entrance ramp and speed onto the highway, outsmarting the schmucks blindly heeding the lazy, state-prescribed route.

Joey and I settle into our seats. The tension drains from our hunched shoulders. It is a beautiful August day, and we are on our way to Cooperstown.

"Hey," Dad says, motioning from the backseat. "There it is again."

Dunn Tire Park materializes on the left. Soon we are on the same haunted industrial road, heading once more into the downtown business district, nearing restaurants that have begun to stir with lunchtime traffic.

"Can you believe this?" my brother asks.

"Bet you're sorry you didn't drive, Dad."

"No, no. I'm enjoying this," he says. He seems truly unbothered by the fact that he is lost in Buffalo. He didn't always have such patience on road trips.

Mom loved to travel northern Michigan, and she'd lead us on long journeys that to a child amounted to torturous, interminable hours in hot vinyl seats. Dad would drive and Mom would study the state map through her black, rhinestone-encrusted cat-eye glasses, directing him down back roads to small inland lakes with names that promised encounters with nature—Bear Lake, Big Bear Lake, Deer Lake, Wolf Lake, Turtle Lake, Bass Lake—or merely intrigued her. (We once spent a week at Starvation Lake.)

"Let's take Old 27," she would say. "It'll be fun."

Somewhere along the way, Dad would grow tired of half-hour side trips to public-access sites and roadside parks and he would get tense and quiet as Mom suggested a prettier detour. He wouldn't say anything but Mom would act as if he had. "Why are you getting angry?" she would ask. He'd stare out the windshield, annoyed by the question. "I just thought it would be nice," she'd say. There'd be some silence and Mom might straighten the burgundy scarf tied stylishly around her frosted wig and wait for Dad to speak. Finally, in a conciliatory voice he'd say, "I'm just tired," and he would ask Mom where he should turn.

In those days we rode in the backseat.

My brother spots a Visitor's Center in downtown Buffalo. It's in a place called the Market Arcade, a historic building with a grand entranceway beneath a cement buffalo head that is either deformed or has lost some of its features. It looks surprisingly similar to my brother.

"You wanna stop?"

"I dunno."

"Well, I don't care."

"Doesn't matter to me."

A half-mile up the road, we circle back through a maze of one-way streets.

The Arcade is one of those now-stylish, back-from-the-dead places filled with professional offices and boutiques.

"My brother's getting us lunch," I tell the lady at the information counter, nudging my head toward Fera's Sub Shop across the decoratively tiled concourse. "I'm just curious. What's the best way to catch I-90 toward Albany?"

I ask the question in such a manner that she will surely conclude I know several ways to get to Albany and am merely wondering which route she prefers. She pulls out a map, circles a spot, and says, speaking slowly, "You are here." She draws thick, crayonlike lines on the map.

"That's the easiest way," she says.

We depart with sandwiches and sodas, Dad still denying his thirst. I resist the urge to ask him, "Don't you think I'll stop the car if you need to use the restroom?"

Rather, I say, "Maybe we'd actually get to Cooperstown if you drove, Dad."

"Nah, you're doing fine."

"You want me to drive?" Joey wonders.

"Can you eat and drive at the same time?"

He looks at me, bobs his empty head, and then wedges himself behind the steering wheel. We escape Buffalo.

5. Sgt. Stankiewicz's Stories

*"**B**aseball gives every American boy a chance to excel. Not just to be as good as anybody else but to be better. This is the nature of man and the name of the game."*

—Ted Williams at his 1966 induction

Twenty miles out of Buffalo we're recalling last night's Tigers game. They won for a change, Jose Lima beating Ichiro Suzuki and the Mariners. Forty miles out Joey gushes about Riley, his granddaughter who has pumpkin hair, like Grandma Muse. Dad loves nothing better than to hear of Riley's exploits or the adventures of his grandchildren.

"Oh, isn't that great?" he says. "That's really something."

Near Rochester Dad tells of the time in the 1960s when he spent a week at Eastman Kodak School with a coworker who would eat free peanuts at the hotel bar rather than spend his meal allowance. "Boy, was he tight with money," he says. "He used to time it so he'd take a crap at work every day to save a few pennies on flushing the toilet at home."

"Hope he worked weekends."

Approaching the Finger Lakes area, my brother wonders whether Barry Bonds will break Mark McGwire's home-run record. He hopes not, preferring that the McGwire–Sammy Sosa race retain its historical sheen.

"He'll blow it," I say. "Bonds doesn't have a prayer in hell."

After the words pass my lips, I wonder if they are offensive to my brother, given his gold cross. "Prayer in hell." He doesn't react so I guess not. Or maybe he has simply chosen to ignore my words, just as I've chosen not to ask him about his necklace. (It's back underneath his shirt.) The fact that I even notice the phrase "prayer in hell" says something about the potential for his faith to alter how we act around each other.

"It used to be a big deal to hit fifty home runs," Dad says, which gets us talking about Hank Greenberg, who hit 58 the season Dad turned eighteen. He says Greenberg created a stir one September by sitting out Yom Kippur during a pennant drive.

In the van we draw Dad into a tale that he's told dozens of times but never too often. It's 1942. He's a twenty-two-year-old sergeant in the Air Corps, hanging out in the recreation center at Rosecrans Field in Missouri, watching Wednesday-night fights with friends.

"They had a pretty good crowd because there was nothing else to do. I was sitting in the auditorium when this older Irish guy comes up and asks me to fight for our squadron. I weighed about one-sixty and they needed somebody in that weight class. At the last minute this other guy backed out of the fight and they didn't have nobody else. I said, 'Heck, I've never been in the ring in my life.' Well, the man said I'd be fine and some of the guys encouraged me. 'Come on, Sergeant Stankiewicz—for the good of the squadron.' "

Dad dressed for the battle and must have appeared fit in the ring for when his opponent saw him he said, "You look like a pro." The other boxer was intimidated. Dad fought like the untrained amateur that he was, pulling his fist way back and telegraphing his punches.

"You get a good fighter and he'd poke your nose twenty-five times before you delivered that punch. But this guy was scared. He went down on the first blow. He got up again. I whacked him down. I knocked him down seven times and he never hit me once. I was so tired by the end of the round that I could hardly breathe."

Dad won on a technical knockout. He bloats his chest in mock pride as he tells the story. "Guys were saying, 'You've really got a punch. Boy you've got some power.' They got me all hyped up. I started thinking, heck, I do have some talent."

A week later Dad accepted an invitation to train at the base gym.

"A Mexican kid one hundred and five or one hundred and six pounds came over and said, 'Sarge, can you spar with me?' I looked at him. He was just a little guy, fifty or sixty pounds lighter than me. I said, 'I'd like to spar with you but I've got a knockout punch. I don't want to hurt you.' He said, 'I move pretty fast, Sarge. I'll take my chances. Maybe I'll learn something.' "

Dad humored the flyweight. He'd spar with him but would take it easy and maybe the kid would learn something.

"He was jumping around in the ring and he began peppering

me in the nose, not hard but over and over again. So I decided to hit him, but not with my killer strength. I swung one of my telegraph punches but he wasn't nowhere near when it arrived and he got in another six or seven punches on my nose. The kid was saying, 'Am I hurting you, Sarge? Am I hurting you?' "

Dad's laughing by this point, as are we.

"He popped me in the nose again and again. 'Am I hurting you, Sarge?' Meanwhile, I'm getting mad as hell.

" 'Am I hurting you, Sarge?' "

Joey glances in the rearview mirror. Dad is fully in character, animated and grimacing and shaking his head and growling out his words. Dad's got a bit of ham in him. In school he starred in stage productions. It's something I didn't know until adulthood when I stumbled upon a yellowed program in one of his scrapbooks.

" 'No, you're not hurting me,' " Dad yells. "I figured it was time to end it so I started swinging wildly at full strength and he kept pummeling my nose and I kept missing and I started bleeding. That's when I learned I shouldn't fight, from that little Mexican guy."

We're all gut laughing as Dad concludes his tale of humility.

"The next week the guys from Rosecrans Field were scheduled to go against black fighters from Fort Riley. Some of those guys were ringers. They could really box. They had a match lined up for me but I refused. I was no boxer."

There's a moment of quiet when Dad finishes, and the words and laughter settle over us. I try in these seconds to imprint the sound of his voice—the telling of the story—on my memory, for there will come a day too soon when that's the only place I'll hear his stories, in my mind. But years from now I will ask my brother, "Remember how excited Dad would get when he'd talk about boxing in the Air Corps?" And we'll both think of this day and our trip.

A long Interstate 90 there's a sign for the National Women's Hall of Fame in Seneca Falls, where in 1848 Lucretia Mott and Elizabeth Cady Stanton held the first women's rights convention.

If we were to go there, we could delicately drop our name— Stanton—and encourage the staff to imagine we are somehow connected to Elizabeth Cady. It would be the equivalent of going to Cooperstown with the last name of Doubleday—well, sort of. Obviously, we wouldn't tell them that my father changed our last name when we were children. (He figured Joey would have an easier time spelling Stanton.)

Located in the columned building of a former bank, the Women's Hall of Fame honors the wide-ranging achievements of inductees like Rosa Parks, Clara Barton, Billie Jean King, Eleanor Roosevelt, Amelia Earhart, and Shirley Chisholm, who ran for president in 1972. It opened forty years after the Cooperstown shrine.

The Baseball Hall of Fame wasn't the nation's first—one in the Bronx recognizing "great Americans" was founded in 1900— but it is the best known and its success unparalleled. Many have tried to duplicate it. In New York state alone there are more than fifteen other halls of fame. They honor dancers and long-distance runners, thoroughbred horses and harness racers, women athletes and fly fishermen, and fiddlers and twirlers and maple-syrup makers. There's a hall of fame for almost everything now.

INTERNATIONAL BOXING HALL OF FAME, says a sign between Syracuse and Utica.

"Dad, you might have made it there if you had kept boxing."

"Oh, no," he says.

The hours and miles disappear in a breeze of words and memories. We leave the toll way at Exit 30 near Herkimer and cross the river into Mohawk, passing a vacant Big M supermarket in a town that has seen more prosperous days.

"Hey, there's a sports card shop," Joey says.

The sighting confirms we are on the right path.

Cooperstown lies thirty to forty minutes from the freeway in the foothills of upstate New York. It's not a convenient, jump-off-the-highway stop. If it were, it would lose much of its charm and attract the mildly curious in search of a thirty-minute diversion. It is better that we must drive through the countryside to get there. It is best that we don't stumble upon it en route to someplace else, that it be a destination, not a serendipitous surprise, that the others who visit it truly yearn to be there, that they also cherish the sport.

The drive builds anticipation. If I were a boy, this stretch might feel intolerable, punctuated by a dozen are-we-there-yets.

From Exit 30 you travel through Mohawk, Dennison Corners, and Richfield Springs, towns so small that if you added their populations the sum would barely equal Ty Cobb's 4,191 alleged hits. In sections the road opens upon grand vistas, where the shadows of puffy clouds move across the landscape. The air is scented with pastures and mown grass and wild flowers. Black-and-white Holsteins graze in meadows and horses meander behind wood fences and in the shade of solitary trees.

Highway 28 follows the shoreline of Canadarago Lake, its two lanes twisting through the tiny communities of Schuyler Lake and Fly Creek. It winds and rolls through hills patched in green and past low gray walls of stone and alongside blockish, two-story homes precariously close to the pavement. In one yard there are yellow flower planters made from tractor tires that have been turned inside out and sliced decoratively. In another, a homemade sign warns, JESUS OR HELL. YOUR CHOICE.

Weathered, unpainted barns lean toward the road like hunched old men. They look as if they might collapse under the weight of next winter's snow. The buildings are humble, some undoubtedly survivors from the 1800s, and they help you imagine that you are traveling through time, beyond your and your brother's childhoods, beyond your father's boyhood, even your grandfather's.

Up ahead a squirrel crosses the road in front of us. I slow and beep the horn and it scampers toward the shoulder.

Nearer Cooperstown are antique markets and quilt stores and motels with names like Major League Motor Inn. The houses become progressively more pampered with painted shutters and groomed yards. The last stretch of Highway 28 heads downhill beneath a canopy of trees. The roadway is dappled with sunlight and shade, and a sign welcomes, COOPERS-TOWN. HOME OF BASEBALL. VILLAGE OF MUSEUMS.

"We made good time," my brother says.

"Considering you don't know how to read a map."

He snorts. "I'm not the one who drove to Toronto."

"No, you navigated us through Buffalo—three times."

We come in on Chestnut Street amid Victorian inns, houses with plaques, and bed-and-breakfasts more colorful than Enos Cabell's Astro jersey. It is mid-afternoon, and the streets have traffic, though not congestion. We've beaten the rush of Induction Weekend when the biggest crowds of the year come to see the Hall enshrine its new members. For those honored, membership in that select fraternity is often the highlight of a lifetime.

It is busier on Main Street, which is lined with trees, baseball-themed businesses, and black street lamps that hark back to another time. Baskets of red geraniums hang throughout, and a flagpole stands at Main and Pioneer in the center of the intersection, encircled in cement.

Hot air rushes through our car windows.

"The hotel is over there, Dad." I point toward Lake Otsego.

Up the block on the right people gather on the sidewalk outside a two-story red-brick building with paned windows and arched entranceways and a banner in our flag's colors proclaiming Bill Mazeroski, Kirby Puckett, Hilton Smith, and Dave Winfield as the latest honorees. The place looks as American as anything in Philadelphia.

It is the Hall of Fame, the National Baseball Hall of Fame and Museum.

"We're finally here," Dad says.

I had no idea in 1972 that it would take so long.

6. May 1972: Wee Willie Keeler's Advice

Billy Martin's Tigers began May in first place, just ahead of the Orioles, with Mickey Lolich vying for the league lead in victories. "I'm not in the groove yet," Lolich said. "I'm going to get better. I know I'm not myself yet. I'm having trouble getting my slider where I want it and my fastball is a little erratic. Last year, every time I threw I knew where the pitch was going to end up."

Lolich won his third game in late April, derailing Wilbur Wood's perfect 3-0 record. The White Sox knuckleballer had surrendered one run in thirty-six innings. The victory tied Lolich with Wood, teammate Joe Coleman, and Bert Blyleven. But a younger star whom many expected to see atop the list had yet to appear in a game.

ABOVE: The author and friend Jeff Mancini

Vida Blue, Lolich's nemesis, had become entangled in a contract dispute with his boss, A's owner Charlie Finley. Blue sat out the first month of the season for more money. He had made $14,750 in his Cy Young season and wanted a raise to $92,000. Finley was offering $50,000.

"They're both crazy," Dad said. At the time he was making $16,000.

It's understandable why a kid consumed by baseball would dream of going to Cooperstown. It's the logical next step after you've been following the game passionately in the *Sporting News*, reading Joe Falls's and Bob Broeg's columns, and after you've been tuning to WJR every weeknight just before 8 P.M. for Ernie Harwell's pregame show and after you've been collecting all the Topps cards your allowance will allow and have been going to the ballpark as many times as possible and have seen your Tigers play a benefit basketball game against teachers at a nearby school. After that, Cooperstown is what remains.

That part's understandable. What's more difficult to comprehend is how the dream of going grabbed hold of me and never loosened its grip. It wasn't something that I mentioned occasionally that year. From the moment my father said that "maybe" we'd go to the Hall of Fame, I talked about it all the time. I talked about it at school in Mr. Harla's gym class while waiting for the bell to ring. I talked about it while shagging fly balls at St. Malachy practices and over Dad's meatloaf dinners at home and during Miss Itkin's lectures about Spanish explorers. Until finally I met someone who had been to Cooperstown.

Unfortunately, it was Blythe Topelsky.

"I saw everything," he bragged to a group of kids over pizza burgers in the Melby Junior High cafeteria. Blythe was a showy, sidearm-throwing fastball pitcher who dominated our league. Cocky and charismatic, he ingratiated himself to teachers— despite his smart mouth, his propensity for reciting the alphabet by burp, and his habit of lacerating other kids verbally for no reason.

"The Hall of Fame is unbelievable," he said. "They have everything there. Babe Ruth's bat, Mickey Mantle's glove, Ty Cobb's shoes. Everything. It's fantastic. That's where I'm going to be someday. In the Hall of Fame."

There was no arguing his logic because Blythe played baseball better than I did and I certainly planned to be inducted in Cooperstown. So I supposed he would be, too. For a brief moment I thought we had something in common, that maybe he wasn't so bad after all.

"I'm going there this summer," I said.

Topelsky rolled his eyes at the other kids around the table. "Yeah, Stanton. Sure," he said. "The only way you're going to Cooperstown is on a special bus for stupid retards."

My father came from work one day with a black hardcover book titled, in bold red letters, *The Story of Baseball*. The cover resembled the page of a photo album, with action shots of Stan Musial, The Great Ted Williams, and Willie Mays cropped and bordered to look like Polaroids. The subtitle proclaimed it "a completely illustrated and exciting history of America's national game." It contained a wealth of material with which I could pad endless conversations. On those 191 pages were stories and pictures that gave life to the names that Dad had been dropping.

There was Mickey Cochrane, crouching in catcher's gear, minus the mask, with his cap on backwards and his big ears protruding. There was smiling Pepper Martin of the Gas House Gang, with hawk nose and unshaven face, punching his wadded glove, and Casey Stengel doffing his cap as his players hoisted him after winning the pennant, and Joe DiMaggio chatting with a young Mickey Mantle on the dugout steps. And there were Babe Ruth photos throughout, crossing the plate for his 60th home run, posing with Yankee mascot Ray Kelly, shaking hands with Miller Huggins after one of their feuds, embracing Lou Gehrig near the end, and swinging in all his glory, the camera near the ground and pointed upward, showing his backside, the number three set against pinstripes, his torso twisted toward first, his head angled at the right-field stands, looking more majestic than a Yankee has a right to, looking as heroic as only he could.

Near the back of the book were the men whose plays I had witnessed: Brooks diving, Gibson delivering, Yaz hitting, Mays flashing that wide smile, and Lolich leaping into the arms of Bill Freehan after Game Seven of the 1968 Series. But what intrigued me more were the unfamiliar stories, of Rube Waddell, a sometimes brilliant player with crazy eyes and childish demeanor who according to author John Rosenburg chased after the clanging bells of a fire engine when he should have been on the mound pitching; of Judge Kenesaw Mountain Landis, a craggy-faced man who ruled baseball during the Black Sox Scandal; of Mordecai "Three Finger" Brown, who though maimed in a farming accident had legendary battles with Christy Mathewson; of Wee Willie Keeler—how could a kid not be intrigued by the name alone?—and his teammate John Mc-Graw, whom Rosenburg described as "runty" and who as a boy drove his parents "to distraction" with his love for baseball. The book, with its up-to-date list of Hall of Famers, felt like a preview of good things to come. It was an unspoken pledge from my father, a promise that we would be going to Cooperstown.

Optimism abounds in spring. The lawn emerges from its brown sleep, trees bud, robins nest, the forsythia bush ignites with yellow leaves, and our youth-league coaches call us to practice. It's a glorious time to be a kid.

Coach Ed Rychlewski looked a little like Curly of the Three Stooges, with his rounded physique and nearly shaven head. He even had a bit of Curly's good nature, but a whole lot more smarts. Coach grew up in the coal-mining country of northeast Pennsylvania in the small town of Larksville, across the Susquehanna River from Wilkes-Barre where the Barons of the Eastern League played. As a boy he rooted for the Cleveland Indians rather than the closer Phillies or Yankees because of the Indians' ties to the local farm club and his allegiance to former Barons like Bob Lemon, Luke Easter, and "Suitcase" Simpson.

That was long before I met him in the spring of '72. By then he had eight children, a life in Michigan, and a year or two under his belt as assistant coach of our St. Malachy Tigers, for whom his oldest son, Eddie, pitched left-handed and played second base. Though Mr. Szydlak, a wiry man with black, Bryl-creemed hair, actually managed the team, Coach Rychlewski did a share of the instructing. We practiced two or three times a week before the start of the season, fielding grounders, catching flies, and rehearsing bunts, cut-offs, and double plays. "If you get to practice, you get to play," he said.

One afternoon he gathered us fifth and sixth graders around home plate. There were miniature valleys on each side where players had been digging themselves in against pitchers. He etched a batter's box into the sand with the tip of his tennis shoe and demonstrated a proper stance, showing us to stride into a pitch and repeating the mantra of youth coaches around the world: "Keep your eye on the ball." Then he quizzed us, calling us by our last names in his playfully brusque manner.

"So Stanton, if you want to get a hit what do you have to do?"

"You hit 'em where they ain't," I said.

Jeff Mancini made a face as if sucking on a sour-apple Jolly Rancher.

I repeated, "Wee Willie Keeler said, 'You hit 'em where they ain't.' "

"Willie who?" someone asked.

I looked at Coach Rychlewski, who was smirking, and explained: "Wee Willie Keeler played for the Baltimore Orioles in the 1890s. He's in the Hall of Fame."

"You donkey!" he said. "I know who Keeler was." He squinted at me and shook his head. "And he's not here right now. . . . You have to keep your eye on the ball. You can't hit what you can't see. Keep . . . your eye . . . on the ball."

It wasn't the answer he wanted; it was better. I had elevated myself above the others. I wasn't just a kid who could name Cash or Kaline or Hank Aaron. I could invoke the legend of a long-dead dead-ball hitter, and that was worth something.

As a child you learn quickly that your fascination with baseball, while peculiar to some, endears you to others. It instantly bridges decades, connecting you to older fans with whom you might otherwise have nothing in common. You find yourself at family gatherings gravitating toward the uncles who bubble about the time they saw Jimmie Foxx or Lou Gehrig or Walter Johnson; you find yourself striking up conversations with the teacher who in class drops Duke Snider's name, or with the allergist whose waiting room features the Norman Rockwell print of umpires looking skyward for rain.

After practice Coach Rychlewski and Mr. Szydlak stood in the parking lot by an open car trunk, drinking beers from a cooler.

"Wee Willie Keeler?" he said, as I rode by on Jeff's handlebars. "How about Dale Mitchell? You ever hear of him? Golly, that guy could hit."

On the way home Jeff and I gloated about what each of us had done well at practice and how we were almost good enough for the Tigers already.

"My dad's gonna take me to Cooperstown this summer," I told Jeff. "Maybe you can come with us."

The promise cast an ebullient glow over our conversation.

We talked about his dad's upcoming races and some driver's latest funny-car entry. We pondered the grotesque and the unusual, the things that entertained boys our age: the Bermuda

Triangle, UFOs, the double-jointed kid on the next block who could pull his thumb backward and touch it to his wrist; how to kill a guy by karate-chopping the bridge of his nose and jamming it back into his brain with the palm of your hand; or how somebody's brother a few streets over had been "blown away" in Vietnam.

"Won't Joey get to fight?" Jeff asked.

"Not till he's out of school."

"Ain't he scared?"

"No way! He's already got an Army jacket."

I told him how my brother was tough, how he used to be a fast running back for the Melby Rebels and how he'd be playing football for the Cousino High Patriots if he weren't so busy with other things.

"He's stronger than he looks," I said.

On a midweek afternoon, Dad and Joey—home from work and school—grabbed their gloves and a ball and ventured into the front yard for a game of running bases. It happened so rarely anymore, the three of us playing in the creeping shade of the birch tree, that even then I knew to savor it.

Our sun-christened neighborhood brimmed with life that day, drawing kids outdoors and away from their homework and the *Little Rascals* reruns on the UHF station. Down the block Mr. Woitha pushed his mower cheerfully over his thick lawn and around his evergreen, and Mrs. Metts pulled weeds from her garden. Randy, across the street, tinkered with his mag-wheeled Thunderbird, revving it not far from where Colleen played hopscotch with the Burchette sisters on the sidewalk outside their home. Jody, the black lab next door, was barking to be set free from the Knudsens' yard.

"I'll catch but I'm not going to run," my brother said. He didn't want to get sweaty. He had plans to go out that night with his friends and discuss the significance of "Maggie May"— or something like that, I imagined.

Dad stood at the edge of our driveway in his steel-toed work shoes and Joey stood at the start of our neighbor's in his sandals, sixty feet of sidewalk and a world of space between them. They looked so different, one in bell-bottom jeans and wire-rim glasses, with light hair falling to the shoulders, the other in brown polyester slacks and a patterned short-sleeved shirt, wavy black hair combed back, sideburns short and graying. One worked at the tank plant; the other protested outside it.

They lobbed the ball as a pack of kids—me, Jeff, Mark, and Ron-Ron Mancini, Jimmy the Exhibitionist—darted chaotically from driveway to driveway, trying to avoid the tag.

Though Joey no longer dressed like an athlete and had stopped following the sport after painting his bedroom yellow and black and decorating it with protest posters imprinted with marijuana leaves, he could catch and throw. And Dad still possessed the smooth motion of an athlete. As a teen he had broken up a Hal Newhouser no-hitter, one year before Newhouser made it to the majors.

Joey and Dad missed the ball mostly when they chose, bobbling it and dropping it on close plays and throwing pop-ups to keep the game exciting for the younger kids who had no clue when to run and frequently took off in the same direction as the ball.

Jeff Mancini and I knew better.

"I'm Joe Morgan," he said.

"I'm Lou Brock," I countered, quickly switching to my Howard Cosell voice. "Brock takes a tremendous lead at first."

Dad, standing beside our gas lamp, held the ball in his throwing hand.

Jeff edged away from the bag and toward him. Dad flung the white tennis ball to Joey, using mostly his wrist. We took off. Joey fired to Dad, trapping us in a rundown. The younger kids joined in and in the bedlam that followed, I escaped by faking a change in direction as Dad flipped the ball to my brother.

"Brock's safe at second!" Cosell exclaimed.

"Brock?" Dad replied, his eyes happier than usual. "You sure that wasn't Gee Walker?"

I thought it was a compliment. Actually, though, Walker had been picked off during a crucial rally in the 1934 Series and numerous other times. He was easily distracted when opposing players called him names. Against the Yankees and Red Ruffing, he even fell for the hidden-ball trick. But I didn't know that then.

I basked in my success, ducking and dancing and feeling rightly proud.

"Boy, I wish I had your energy," Dad said.

It was a raucous game.

On one play I dove headfirst beside the sidewalk, the grass halting my slide.

"Pete Rose?" asked Dad.

Normally the goal was to steal ten bases and earn the right to catch. But with Joey refusing to surrender the glove I aspired to something else, to impress Dad and my brother with my talent, to dazzle them with my speed, to help them see my infinite abilities, to draw their genuine admiration. Such naked pursuit of their attention flows like a river through my life. I wanted to make my father so proud he would erupt in praise and bestow upon me a banquet of accolades and right then and there set the date for our Hall of Fame trip. "Boy, he's really good," I imagined him thinking. "Cooperstown, here we come."

And I wanted my brother to see me as a peer, as someone closer to his age, and to realize that I was no longer a little kid. I hoped he might invite me along with his friends. We could talk about "Maggie May"—and Billy Martin.

The game, the sun, the attention, being the star in their eyes—it felt so right. It seemed on that afternoon as if Joey had forgotten all about the Vietnam War and as if Dad had escaped his worry over Mom's next brain surgery.

7. Cooperstown at Last

> " 'So who was Cooperstown named after?' he
> says, facing toward the sparkling lake as if it
> were a space he were considering flying off into.
>   " 'James Fenimore Cooper,' I say. 'He was a
> famous American novelist who wrote books
> about Indians playing baseball.' Paul flashes me
> a look of halfway pleasant uncertainty. He
> knows I'm tired of him and may be making fun
> of him again."
>
> —Frank Bascombe talking to his son, Paul, in
> Richard Ford's novel *Independence Day*

Children in baseball uniforms and parents in ball caps—San Francisco, Minnesota, St. Louis, the Houston Colt .45s—bustle along the sidewalks of Cooperstown. There are babies in strollers and a man with implausibly black hair and matching wraparound cataract sunglasses. There is a bus ahead waiting for the errant members of a tour group to reappear. There's a kid yelling across the street, toward Mickey's Place, "Mom's looking for you!" Near an information kiosk, a young man in a Marilyn Manson T-shirt kicks a Hacky Sack ball. Cars are parked all along Main Street, diagonally on one side, parallel on the other, as if the town can't agree on what's best—a local debate of designated-hitter proportions.

"It takes more skill to parallel park," I imagine one side arguing.

"Maybe," counters the other, "but diagonal parking means more spaces and that's what people want. More spaces. Give them more spaces."

Most of the structures along Main Street were built in the 1800s. One, the Nancy Williams House, dates to 1797. The downtown features three-story buildings with street-level stores that have large window displays, recessed doors, and flower boxes. There are tasteful shutters, fancy brickwork, and intricate cornices. Stand with your back to the gray vinyl-sided CVS pharmacy that somehow slipped into the bench-aplenty streetscape and you'll appreciate that this village has a rich heritage. Two families—the Coopers and the Clarks—and one Civil War general, Abner Doubleday, shaped the history of Cooperstown, the former by actions, the last in myth. Their impact—real and imagined—is felt yet.

In the late 1700s, three years before George Washington ascended to the presidency, William Cooper founded the town. He carved it from wilderness along the south end of nine-mile Otsego Lake and lured settlers who hoped to make their livings producing maple sugar and ash products. In 1790 Cooper moved his family into a manor house that he had built on land that now borders the Hall of Fame. The home burned in the fire of 1853 but a statue of his famous author-son, streaked and green with age, marks the location on Cooper Grounds, a rolling landscape fenced with wrought iron.

An ambitious, rough-edged man, William Cooper improved his standing in society, rising from wheelwright to land speculator, congressman, and judge. According to Pulitzer Prize–winning historian Alan Taylor, Cooper prospered with his town.

In time, however, after residents rejected his brand of federalism in favor of populism, Cooper lost power and prestige. After his death, his fortune evaporated, prompting his youngest son to pursue a career in literature.

James Fenimore Cooper became one of the country's best-known novelists, mining his village days for the frontier stories that made him required reading in high schools and colleges across America: *The Pioneers, The Last of the Mohicans, The Pathfinder,* and *The Deerslayer*.

Although Cooperstown has become synonymous with baseball, it also embraces its most well-known native and his characters. There are memorials, an art museum that carries his name, a state park called Glimmerglass (his pseudonym for Lake Otsego), and myriad businesses that pay homage to his works: Deerslayer Lodge, Mohican Flowers, Pathfinder Realty, Pioneer Wine and Spirits, and Leatherstocking Golf Course. Some streets even carry those names.

The author's later years in the village overlapped with those of Abner Doubleday and Edward Clark.

Doubleday had family in the area and was schooled locally in the 1830s before heading to West Point and embarking on a military career. He served in the Mexican War, reportedly fired the first Union shot at Fort Sumter, and commanded men at Antietam, Fredericksburg, and Gettysburg, where a statue honors him. In retirement by some accounts, he helped start the first cable-car company in San Francisco. Doubleday distinguished himself with legitimate successes but ironically most people remember him best for what he did not do: invent baseball.

Fourteen years after Doubleday's 1893 death, the Mills Commission, initiated by sportsman Albert Spalding—who wanted to document his belief that baseball was a uniquely American creation—proclaimed Doubleday father of the sport. The commission, headed by former National League President Abraham Mills, based its findings on a letter from Abner Graves, an elderly man who recalled that in 1839 (when Graves was five) Doubleday, then twenty, transformed the British game of Town Ball into what would become the national pastime. Graves said that Doubleday introduced the baseball diamond that summer in Cooperstown.

Numerous holes exist in Graves's contention, starting with the fact that Doubleday was at West Point in 1839. Further, though he kept detailed journals and wrote extensively, Doubleday never mentioned baseball in his papers. More importantly, a version of the sport was being played elsewhere earlier. Most historians believe that baseball evolved from other games in the early to mid-1800s. Anymore, no one seriously argues that Doubleday played a role in its creation, not even authorities at the Hall of Fame, which has its roots in the Doubleday myth.

"As we like to say here," explains an official, "if the game wasn't invented in Cooperstown it should have been."

The town might never have become host to the Hall of Fame if not for the Singer sewing machine. Its inventor, Isaac Singer, enlisted the assistance of attorney Edward Clark in 1848, and the two men became business partners. Clark had a knack for marketing. He hatched the idea of selling sewing machines to ministers' wives at half price, knowing that the machines would create demand among other women in the congregations. Clark also helped popularize installment plans, and even built the Dakota apartment building in New York.

He amassed a fortune, and his family later shared it through generous philanthropic efforts in Cooperstown. In the mid-1930s—with Doubleday Field already established—Clark's grandson Stephen bought an archaic stitched baseball that had been discovered in an attic trunk in nearby Fly Creek. The trunk reportedly belonged to Abner Graves, and some theorized that Abner Doubleday had used the ball—and so was born another myth. Clark displayed his five-dollar purchase, the "Doubleday Ball," at the village hall. He and employee Alexander Cleland began pursuing the potential for a national museum for the sport. With backing from professional baseball, particularly National League President Ford Frick, the museum was incorporated—and the idea expanded to include a hall of fame. Among the first directors was James Fenimore Cooper, grandson of the novelist. In 1939 the shrine opened, dedicated on the erroneous centennial of Doubleday's by-then-debunked invention. In their most optimistic dreams, the founders could not have fathomed what the place would come to mean to generations of fans.

Thousands witnessed the first induction, crowding the same section of Main Street that Dad, Joey, and I occupy today.

It's late afternoon, and we should check in at the hotel. But how do you drive past the Hall of Fame and not stop when the place rises before your eyes right along the sidewalk? Seeing it in person after almost thirty years of imagining it in boyhood fantasies reminds me of how I felt as a child when we'd go to

Tiger Stadium. I'd dart up and down the ramps and through the tunnels, salivating over the miniature bats at the souvenir stands and waving wildly at the players on the field, hoping to be noticed. I'd be bouncing in the seat, my feet tapping the concrete floor, my mind racing, praying that the game would go into extra innings, fifteen innings, eighteen innings, that we would stay late into the night, that by some miracle we'd win a contest and get tickets to every game. The thrill of it coursed through me.

We step out of the minivan into the humidity. The sidewalk is stirring with activity. Dozens mill outside the entranceway, some at the museum's Standings Board, which shows the Tigers in fourth place in the AL Central. You can almost hold the good cheer that permeates this Rockwellian place. There's nothing like the sense of shared joy, the genuine feeling of community, that comes when you're among others who also have traveled hours—and years—on their own disjointed journeys.

For a moment we simply stand and stare in silence.

It's different than I had imagined. I had pictured it on the other side of the street, set back a hundred yards or so, atop a gentle hill with a huge grassy promenade leading to the front door and a mammoth parking lot on one side. But it's right along the road, butting up against the sidewalk, and the parking spots are the same ones used for the general store next door and the post office across the street.

I thought the sight of the place might instantly send my mind swimming back to school days, to spring mornings on sandlots, to sunny afternoons with the St. Malachy squad. But that wave of nostalgia doesn't break until I spot a small plaque next to what used to be the main entrance. SITE OF THE FIRST NATIONAL BASEBALL HALL OF FAME INDUCTION. JUNE 12, 1939. ATTENDED BY GROVER ALEXANDER, TY COBB, EDDIE COLLINS, WALTER JOHNSON, NAP LAJOIE, CONNIE MACK, BABE RUTH, GEORGE SISLER, TRIS SPEAKER, HONUS WAGNER, AND CY YOUNG.

Legends. Old legends. Most of them played professional ball when Dad was a boy, some before my grandfather had immigrated from Poland. By 1960, the year I was born, only two of those men—Cobb and Sisler—remained alive and Cobb lasted just another year. But for those who immersed themselves in baseball—whether in the 1940s, the 1970s, or even the 2000s—those names evoke a glorious history.

Dad turns toward me but says nothing.

None of us wants to rush in and push our way through the exhibits.

Instead we seek out Dale Petroskey, who cofounded the Mayo Smith Society, a Tiger fan organization. When Petroskey became president of the Hall of Fame, he invited society members to stop by his office when in Cooperstown. Of course, he probably didn't think any of us would do so on the busiest week of his year. But we try.

The atmosphere inside the administrative entrance is subdued and dignified, like a nice law office, only with framed baseball photos on the walls. I was thinking Stan Musial or Willie Mays might be lingering at the front desk. But they're not, and as it turns out, neither is Dale Petroskey. He's at the Otesaga Hotel welcoming baseball's most famous athletes.

Scot Mondore, who manages museum programs, greets us.

"Anyone ever tell you how lucky you are to work here?"

"Every day," he says.

The museum employs seventy or eighty people full-time year-round, twice that in summer. Most who hold administrative positions moved to the area for their jobs. Mondore, thirty-three, did not. He grew up in Richfield Springs, down the street from a Little League field. The sounds of the game—kids yelling, cheers rising, an occasional crisp hit—filled his summers. His dad, a Mets fan, had a job that kept him on the road, so his mom, who as a girl took the train to see games at Yankee Stadium and Ebbets Field, taught him to play catch and instilled in him a love for the sport and the team in the Bronx.

When you're raised in the Otsego area, you learn about the revered Hall of Fame. It draws thousands through your community, and it gives work to people you know—including, in Mondore's case, his great uncle Ham.

Every summer in the mid- and late-1970s, Mondore visited his uncle's home in Cooperstown. A short guy with a big gut and buzz cut, Uncle Ham worked in maintenance at the Hall of Fame. His desk was in the basement near the archives. "He would let me see some of that stuff," says Mondore. "But it's not like I was swinging Babe's bat or playing catch with Gehrig's glove."

Mondore hung out at the museum while his uncle worked. He wandered the exhibits, listening on a telephone to the recorded voice of Babe Ruth reminiscing about his called shot in 1932. He memorized Abbott and Costello's "Who's on First?" routine and later lingered over the posthumous tribute to Thurman Munson, one of his idols.

"I've come here my whole life," Mondore says.

When he turned eighteen, he joined the military. Every time he came home, he visited the museum. He watched it change and grow. He viewed it as a treasured part of his past, part of who he was, not who he would become. In the Cooperstown region unless you're a doctor at Bassett Hospital—another institution started by the Clarks—there aren't many ways to make a lucrative living. Early on, that's what Mondore wanted. He earned a degree in accounting and pursued another in economics. Yet, all along he felt drawn to the place where he had spent so much time. In college he took a class in sports history and became intrigued by the Negro Leagues and Jackie Robinson, which prompted him to reconsider his ambitions.

He landed an internship at the Hall of Fame in his mid-twenties. Every morning he'd arrive an hour-and-a-half before the museum opened and walk through the silent gallery of plaques, his shoes sounding on the floor. Mondore would acknowledge the men on the walls. Some, like Reggie Jackson and Rod Carew, he had seen play. But most recalled other eras. George Wright had been with Boston in 1876 when Custer died at Little Big Horn; Samuel Thompson, with his walrus mustache, had been a veteran of eleven seasons when presidential candidate William Jennings Bryan delivered his Cross of Gold speech; Cy Young had given his best years on the mound by the time of the San Francisco earthquake; Ty Cobb had already led the league in hitting five times when the Titanic sank; and Babe Ruth was on his way to 60 home runs when Charles Lindbergh was on his way to Paris. The men enshrined in the hall represent a broad stroke of history, predating the Civil War and continuing through the Great Depression, World War II, Kennedy's assassination, Vietnam, the Bicentennial, and my crush on Tatum O'Neal of *The Bad News Bears*.

Mondore stayed after the internship. Over the years his responsibilities and credentials have grown. At the opening of the Pride and Passion exhibit, he met Jackie Robinson's widow, Rachel, and introduced his wife and two daughters to her. It stands as one highlight among many. But the upcoming festivities excite him as well.

"This weekend is my Christmas," he says. "Hall of Fame Weekend."

Cooperstown buzzes. The hotels fill, parking spaces disappear, and trolleys stream through the village, ferrying guests to attractions. Though open year-round, the Hall of Fame draws most of its 300,000 to 400,000 visitors between Memorial Day and Veteran's Day, and many of them come for the big weekend when new members get inducted. Two years ago 50,000 people witnessed the enshrinement of Nolan Ryan, George Brett, and Robin Yount. The turnout won't be as big this weekend but no one here will doubt what time of year it is.

"This induction will be my eighth," says Mondore. "Every year I'm so thrilled to be here with these Hall of Famers. I just sit and let them talk. I love this place."

We leave for the Tunnicliff Inn, up the block and around the corner.

8. Ease Its Pain

> **"L**adies and gentlemen, we come now to the
> conclusion of one of the most elaborate and brilliant
> ceremonies that sportsdom has ever known. Here in
> the slumbering little city of Cooperstown, located in
> upstate New York, thousands of persons have come
> from the four corners of this country to be here today
> to rub elbows with these immortals of baseball. . . .
> The password of the day seems to be this, 'Give your
> boy a ball and a bat with which to play and your
> worries will be over that he might go astray.' "
>
> —Tom Manning reporting for NBC Radio at the 1939
> Hall of Fame opening

You up for a walk, Dad?"

We've checked into the hotel. According to the weathered coat-of-arms that hangs from the building, the inn was
established in 1802, seventeen years before Abner Doubleday
entered this world. William Cooper dominated village politics
then, and he counted among his enemies Joseph Tunnicliff,
whose descendants once ran the inn. Tunnicliff irritated Cooper
by refusing to support the candidates he endorsed.

About the walk: Dad hikes more miles than my brother and
I combined. He lives in a small town, New Baltimore, and regularly logs a mile or so to and from the library. He doesn't stroll,
either. He's no Sparky Anderson, studying his shuffling feet as
he approaches the mound to extract a pitcher. He walks with
determination, keeping a steady pace, his eyes aimed ahead. He

used to put in four or five miles a day several times a week on nature trails. So walking is not a problem.

We make our way through memorabilia stores on Main Street that despite their inflated prices enchant us with their offerings. Some resemble a great-grandfather's attic, with an eclectic mix of photos and cards and nineteenth-century games and lumpy gloves. Some specialize in T-shirts and jerseys, some in players like Mantle and Rose. Some make bats on which you can get your own signature engraved. One sells only Christmas ornaments.

At Pioneer and Main we come upon Augur's Books.

A book store, hmm.

"Is it in the window?" my brother asks.

Two dozen books are charmingly displayed in the front windows of this corner store. There's Yogi Berra's latest and Al Stump's *Ty Cobb* biography and Eliott Asinoff's *Eight Men Out*. But there is no copy of Tom Stanton's *The Final Season* to halt passersby. That sweet sepia-tone cover featuring a fine, venerable park is not in the showcase. Undoubtedly an oversight.

"Maybe they have a stack inside," Joey says.

But there is no stack.

"Did you check the shelves?"

I scan the hundreds of book spines that face the aisles, searching for answers.

"Ah, son," says Lawrence Ritter's *The Glory of Their Times*. "I'll tell you how it was. I got published back in '66 and haven't been out of print since. Those were the days. Every book in every store. Multiple copies, too. All of them on display in the window."

"Pure poppycock," says George Will's *Men at Work*. "Allow me to absolve you of your sentimental notions. Where the market is concerned, there is no room for misty-eyed misconceptions."

"Ease its pain . . ."

"Psst, over here," says Jim Bouton's *Ball Four*. "Want in on a secret? There's a peephole in this shelf. Check it out. The book's on the other side and, oh, what a cover."

"Ease its pain . . ."

What was that? Kinsella's *Shoeless Joe*?

"If you move it, it will sell."

That's it. Move the book. Rearrange the shelves. Make it so the cover shows. Sneak it into the window display. No, that's too much. But place it prominently.

I take the lone copy of my book, *The Final Season,* and arrange it so it faces the weary shopper. My brother has done the same at other stores. My friends, as well. And now you, too, faithful reader, are empowered to do so. Store managers don't mind. All authors do it. You should see Stephen King work the stores when his new books come out. He crisscrosses state after state in his rusty 1976 Gremlin, covertly shuffling his books ahead of John Grisham's on storefront counters. It is a sight to behold.

We head off along Main Street away from the Hall of Fame and beneath overcast skies. It's muggy, and we wouldn't mind a sense of the town beyond the stores. But mostly we just want to stretch our legs after a day in a minivan and to burn an hour before dinner.

The tone changes on Chestnut Street amid lush greenery and stately accommodations. On the left stands the historic Inn at Cooperstown, an elegant, three-floor yellow hotel with a long porch dotted with rocking chairs—the kind of place, my brother says, that his wife would love. Across the street behind a pike fence is the colonial Cooper Inn, its shrubs manicured, its exterior covered in greenery, accenting official Hall of Fame welcoming signs. The Clarks, who started the baseball museum, own the inn and several other businesses.

In the parking lot an older couple exits a Lincoln.

"Who's that?"

"Don't recognize him," Joey says.

We presume he's a Hall of Famer. We make that assumption about every man we see who is my father's age, every man old enough to have batted against Hal Newhouser. In truth there aren't many Hall of Famers alive who are my father's age. Babe Ruth died at age fifty-three, Gehrig at thirty-seven, Mantle at sixty-three, Cochrane at fifty-nine. Maybe that's one of the tradeoffs. If you find heaven on earth by playing ball for a living and you perform so brilliantly that the game immortalizes you, then God subtracts a few years. You don't get as long a life.

That seems fair.

Chestnut Street ends at Lake Street. Turn left and follow the road as it winds along Otsego Lake, and you'll come upon The Otesaga, a luxurious resort that requires male patrons wear jackets to dinner. It opened in 1909. Like the adjoining Leatherstocking Golf Course, it is owned by the Clarks. They also helped establish and continue to support the Fenimore Art Museum and the Farmers' Museum, located farther up and across from one another nestled between hills and water.

Along Highway 80, a road sign announces the village. Attached to it is a smaller sign, as orange as a Charlie Finley baseball. It proclaims Cooperstown as home to the 1999 Class C high school state soccer co-champions.

Soccer champions? In Cooperstown?

Months back, the *CoopersTown Crier* reported that the local youth baseball league might have to eliminate one of four teams because of dwindling numbers. "Ever since spring soccer started four or five years ago our numbers have steadily decreased," said a league official.

One reason we come to Cooperstown is to rekindle warm feelings of youthful summer times when baseball was unquestionably the national pastime, when by mid-morning on fields across the continent packs of kids would pick sides and organize themselves into teams and play for hours. We'd like to believe it's still that way. But we know differently. We've seen the vacant ball fields in our own neighborhoods.

I had assumed that Cooperstown, The Baseball Village, would encourage such harmless self-deception, would eradicate any evidence to the contrary. But right in town, across the street and down from the Baseball Hall of Fame, there's a ticket office for the National Soccer Hall of Fame, a modern 30,000-square-foot facility in nearby Oneonta.

On Lake Street off Chestnut is an area of homes where if you ignore the electrical lines and squint at the asphalt until it turns to dirt, you can imagine yourself 150 years back in time. The clapboard houses with their Dutch doors, crooked entranceways, and decorative chimneys evoke another era.

A block up and over is the lake. The haze mutes the green hills in the distance. Those closest to the horizon nearly disappear in a palette of gray.

"Your mum would love this," Dad says.

The water laps at the shoreline.

My brother snaps a photo of the lake and then poses one of Dad and me beside each other. I take one of them, too.

Heading away from Lakefront Park uphill toward Main Street, the walk is steep.

"You okay, Dad?"

"Yep, I'm still okay," he says.

Evidently, I've asked him that question several times.

With Dad in his eighties, I've developed a bad habit of trying to insulate him from anything that might put him in jeopardy, from phone solicitors to traveling roofers. For a while I insisted he let me or my son Zack cut his lawn. Then he started mowing the grass before we arrived. "You're both busy," he said. "I have lots of time. I pace myself. I take breaks. I don't work when it's hot. I don't overdo it. I like being in the yard. I like doing things for myself."

He sounded like me twenty-some years earlier trying to get his permission to drive the car. "I'll be careful. I'll drive slowly. I won't go downtown. I won't stay out late. . . ."

We've compromised. Dad does his own lawn work. I shovel the snow. (That stuff's a heart attack waiting to happen.)

At Main Street is the former village office, built and donated by yet another Clark. Standing two stories with twelve white columns along its front, the building was home to the first baseball museum. It now houses the police department and a library with cushioned living-room chairs, a fireplace, and a mantel spotlighting the works of James Fenimore Cooper.

Across the street is the statue of Cooper outside the Hall of Fame library, anchored on an island in the road. From the museum's side entrance, another statue, of Mudville's Mighty Casey, looks out toward the author. According to some who work at the library, from certain angles it appears as if Cooper is delivering a pitch to Casey.

"Mom, did you get it?" a boy calls out. The kid is straddling the back of a Johnny Podres statue, his arms wrapped around the left-hander's neck. Podres is pitching to Roy Campanella.

The mom snaps a photo.

"Got it," she says.

A block south sits Presbyterian Church, the oldest in town. It was built in 1805 on land given by William Cooper, who is buried nearby. The reason I mention it is this: Its white steeple has a clock on each of four sides, and all show different, incorrect times. The hands don't move—appropriate for Cooperstown, where time tries to stand still.

And if that isn't symbolic enough, consider this: The museum—which embraces the sport's pastoral, small-town imagery, which celebrates its spiritual roots, which insists that those inducted have played by the rules—borders streets named Main, Church, and Fair.

"This place is pretty as a postcard," Dad says.

9. Banks on the Wall

> **"S**purred by the patently false creation myth,
> the Hall of Fame stands in the most
> incongruous and inappropriate locale of a
> charming little town in central New York.
> Incongruous and inappropriate, but somehow
> wonderful. Who needs another museum in the
> cultural maelstroms (and summer doldrums) of
> New York, Boston, or Washington? Why not a
> major museum in a beautiful and bucolic
> setting? . . . I too am quite content to treat the
> myth gently. . . ."
>
> —Stephen Jay Gould
> in "The Creation Myths of Cooperstown"

At a red-clothed table in the corner of a dark restaurant beneath the Tunnicliff Inn, a man who looks like Bill Mazeroski flutters his left hand to make a point during conversation with a bearded dinner companion. I squint at him, comparing his profile to my fuzzy memory of his face on baseball cards. It's tough to tell without the Pirates cap. But if it's Mazeroski, he's put on some pounds.

I'm unsure, though, and can't quiz my brother about my suspicions because a young waiter with a goatee and pierced eyebrow has arrived for our order. He stands to Dad's right, facing his dead ear.

Before the waiter can ask the questions that Dad will not hear—mashed or baked, soup or salad, dressing, something to drink?—Dad tells him what he wants. He points at the evening special and lists his preferences politely but without pausing: "Pork chops, a salad with ranch, and, uh, decaf please."

This place feels old—second oldest building in town, the waiter confirms. Hotel literature describes it as a turn-of-the-century taproom. Locals call it The Pit. It's mostly underground, which gives it the aura of a forbidden den, a hideout, or a cave (with Mazeroski here, a Pirate's cave?). You enter the establishment from the sidewalk, following narrow steps below street level. A bit of daylight sneaks into the two-room haunt from a single window that faces Pioneer Street. The window is not big enough to crawl out of.

The shiny beige, painted-tile ceiling hangs low enough that Mark McGwire would probably bump his head on it. Pipes snake along it and along water-stained walls that predate plumbing. There's an unpretentious, L-shaped pine bar in one corner, and it's occupied by a few locals who are chatting over the TV in the fluttering light of a sitcom rerun. In the next room a stone fireplace dominates one wall. Crossed Scottish swords are mounted above it.

I lean toward my brother, closer to the glowing candle that accents his Bela Lugosi features, and whisper, "I think that's Bill Mazeroski over there."

Joey sneaks a glance. "Yeah, maybe," he says. "I'm not positive."

Dad has his back to the guy. There is no way of drawing him into the mystery without alerting half of the patrons.

"I wonder what Mazeroski's doing here?"

"Eating?" Joey says.

It's not out of the question. Mickey Mantle, Duke Snider, and others supposedly left their marks on these wooden tables. But there are no pictures of them on the walls, not that I see. There are photo groupings pasted to card stock—Martha Stewart would not approve—of ball players being pulled through town hayride-style and of anonymous guys in World War II military uniforms. There are more recent pictures of youth teams, presumably sponsored by the bar, and there is a Coors Light mirror, too.

The décor is a mix of stuff, certainly not what some Madison Avenue consultant would recommend. But it's authentic, and that's where it finds its charm.

My dad gulps his coffee, black, unsweetened, his first drink of the day.

"It was your mum's birthday Tuesday," he says.

Joey nods. "Yeah, it was. What would she have been? Seventy-nine?"

"Yep." Dad pauses as if waiting for a memory to flicker from his mind. "Seventy-nine . . . hard to believe Betty's been gone that long."

Dad does not wallow in memories of Mom. He mentions her often, devoting a sentence here and there, just enough to keep her near but not enough to trap him in the past. He wants to make sure we don't forget her, as if we could. There was a time, after all, when she was the most important woman in all of our lives, the very heartbeat of our family. She's never far from any of our thoughts but especially close to his. He senses her everywhere, in the orange fire of a mountain-ash tree like the one he planted for her on Shawn Drive; in an artist's turpentine; in the perm solution of a beautician; in the pine-scented breeze at a park; in the recipes he recreates faithfully from her handwritten directions on index cards splattered with butter and grease.

The day after she died Dad woke to find a white feather on her pillow. He put it in a box, to which he added other feathers that appeared in the weeks after. He showed us as he discovered them, with barely a word and a curious, almost apologetic expression that said I-know-this-is-crazy-but.

It rekindled a story Mom had told me as a boy when before one of her surgeries I asked if she was going to die. "Everybody dies," she said. "There's no getting around it. But I'm not planning to go anywhere for a long time, so don't worry." Then she told me about Grandpa Roy and the dove.

In 1957 with three days to Christmas, Roy Muse labored for his last breath in Methodist Hospital in St. Joseph, Missouri. In the next room, Mom, thirty-five, kept vigil for her stepfather, the cheerful carpenter who had raised her as his daughter. On that winter Sunday a white dove flew from the wall of Grandpa Roy's room. It flew before her eyes, right through plaster, as real as her wedding ring, flew right through the bricks, out the hospital, soaring into the heavens. She knew then that he had passed. Over the years, if asked, Mom would share that pretty story, mostly with family because she could never be sure how others would treat it.

We all learn to protect the stories that shape our lives.

Dad slides his plate toward us.

"I'm stuffed," he says. "One of you want this?"

There's an extra pork chop. There was a time when he could eat a few pork chops and gnaw the meat off the bones we had left. But his insatiable appetite departed long ago.

"Too much food," he says. "I hate to throw it out."

The alleged Bill Mazeroski and his guest pay their bill and leave while I am in the restroom, where Mr. Cub, Ernie Banks, apparently scrawled his name above a urinal.

When our check arrives, Dad insists on covering it. He's on a fixed income. Joey and I earn good money.

"You have to let me do something," he says.

We argue, though not much.

10. Charlie's Lessons

*"**G**ray-haired men come and drift about. . . .
Those baseballs in the cases are the balls that
many of them never pitched, caught, or hit on a
big-league diamond. The uniforms are the
baseball suits they never wore. The plaques
speak of the records they never broke, the lives
they never led, and the boyhood dreams they
never fulfilled."*

—James T. Farrell in *My
Baseball Diary*, 1957

It's evening, sometime around seven, and the afternoon
crowds have departed the museum. At the turnstile, a gray-
haired usher offers a map and quick overview. There are exhibits around the corner, two floors of displays up the escalator, a
multimedia presentation that begins in seven minutes in the
theater—"You can still catch it"—and plaques straight ahead.
That is where almost everyone begins, in the gallery, which *is*
the Hall of Fame. The rest of the stuff—the hats and balls and
gloves, the artifacts—comprises the museum. There's a library,
too.

The gallery has a plaque for each man inducted, a bronzed
image accented with bats and laurel leaves, a name, teams,
dates of play, and a brief description of feats. It is a solemn,
walk slowly, talk quietly kind of place where light streams from

the heavens through small windows high above. With its black-marble columns and flecked floors, the room has the feel of a mausoleum.

Hall officials tell the story of a child who while touring the gallery loudly pondered the embossed faces. They reminded him of the scene in *The Empire Strikes Back* where the bad guys encase Han Solo. The boy imagined a similar fate had befallen Lefty Grove, Pud Galvin, and the others. They were trapped in bronze. "How do they get them behind the walls?" he asked.

We enter the gallery together, passing and paying little attention to the oil portrait of Stephen Clark, the philanthropist who launched the museum. Though not a fan of baseball, Clark appreciated history and had the foresight to see the economic potential in his beloved town celebrating its reputation as baseball's birthplace. He thought a museum might draw a few hundred visitors a year.

Clark's presence hints at something most don't realize. Many assume that Major League Baseball owns the museum or at least runs and funds it. It does not. The institution has enjoyed some support from the professional leagues but it remains an independent nonprofit with strong ties to the Clark family. Jane Forbes Clark, granddaughter of the founder, serves as chairman of the Hall's board of directors. She is its largest benefactor—and a Yankee fan.

In the gallery, Dad, Joey, and I drift in different directions—Joey looking for someone in particular, Dad pausing to consider each inscription, and me just drinking in the names.

Kiki Cuyler. Red Ruffing. Goose Goslin. Pee Wee Reese. Robin Roberts. Jocko Conlan. Harry Hooper. Dizzy Dean. Dazzy

Vance. King Kelly. Harry Heilmann. Smokey Joe Williams. Satchel Paige. Whitey, Christy, Rabbit, Chick, Chief, Gabby, and the Rubes (Marquard and Waddell). Red, Nap, Red, Cap, Arky, Yogi, and Pie—shortened from Pieface, the moniker given by a storekeeper who knew of Harold Traynor's sweet tooth. Since boyhood I've had a fascination for names that flow from the tongue in musical bursts. To a child's ear, some sounded ancient—Zack Wheat, Mordecai Brown, Denton "Cy" Young, Tyrus Cobb, Tristram Speaker, Kenesaw Landis, Cornelius Mack.

I saw none of those men play. At most I've watched forty inductees on television or in person. How many have I come to know through my father and uncles? Fifty or a hundred more?

All the names are familiar and most carry memories. Bob Gibson reminds of the time Uncle Clem and I sat in front of a cassette recorder and recreated the 1968 World Series from the play-by-play account in a crumbling newspaper. Nolan Ryan recalls no-hitters and Norm Cash walking up to the plate with a table leg instead of a bat—and a game in 1972 when Ryan struck out the first nine men he faced. Wee Willie Keeler conjures Coach Ed; Honus Wagner, a long-ago lust for a valuable cigarette card; Juan Marichal, the high-kick delivery; Roger Bresnahan, winter games of Stratomatic Baseball; and Johnny Bench, those textured, plastic-coated "3D" Kellogg's cards that prompted me to switch from Cocoa Puffs to Frosted Flakes.

"What's that?" a kid asks his dad.

He points to the emblem on Robin Yount's hat.

"That's the Brewers logo. It's an M and a B for Milwaukee Brewers."

"It's ugly," the kid says.

"Well, what are they going to do, put a beer can on his hat?" The kid laughs.

I hear a shutter snap and look to see Joey with his Nikon. He's in front of the plaque of Al Kaline, whose placid eyes point toward Willie Mays, one plaque over. There's a kid in a Nomar Garciaparra jersey near Mays.

Since my brother's birth in 1954, the Tigers have fielded four Hall of Fame players. But only one, Al Kaline, really counts. Larry Doby appeared briefly in the uniform, and Eddie Mathews, though he contributed to two Detroit pennant drives, was a Brave at heart. And Jim Bunning, despite winning most of his games with us, chose to be immortalized as a Phillie and waited until he was in the National League to deliver his famous Father's Day perfect game. We don't think of him as one of ours.

But Kaline was as much a part of Tiger Stadium as the overhang in right field.

You don't get far into The Game exhibit before encountering myth.

The Doubleday Baseball, its Frankenstein stitches popped along two seams, greets you at the entrance, entombed in a respectful carved case, perched on a pedestal, bathed in toasty light. It's the artifact that began the museum in the 1930s. It looks as reverent and authentic as the Declaration of Independence.

A few steps beyond in a black-ceilinged room with the amber ambience of a romantic restaurant, you find mention of

Tinkers, Evers, and Chance, whose poetic reputations as masters of the double play surpassed their true-life talents. Then there's Babe Ruth calling his home run in the 1932 Series. "He once hit a ball with such velocity," wrote Arthur Daley of *The New York Times*, "that it went screaming through the pitcher's legs and went sailing serenely over the head of the center fielder." Ruth was the Mighty Casey of the real world.

I consider myself a well-read baseball fan. I know that Tinkers and Company weren't as fearsome as portrayed in verse—the stats show that—and I realize that much evidence argues against Ruth having called his shot. But like most devoted fans, I enjoy the game's lore and wink at those lovely stories, wanting to believe them.

But my self-image as an informed baseball fan crumbles in the display on Ruth. "Babe Ruth was not an orphan," it says.

"That can't be right, Dad."

For as long as I can remember, I've known that Babe Ruth was an orphan, raised at St. Mary's School, watched over by Brother Mathias. His parents died young, his mother first. Not so, says the museum.

"Did you know that?"

"Not really," Dad says.

He studies Ruth's dark bat.

Babe's neglectful parents surrendered him to St. Mary's. His mother died when he was a teen, and by the time his bartending father was killed Ruth was already with the Red Sox. How could I be so wrong? Did I manufacture the orphan story? Did I find comfort in it as a boy because of my mom's sickness and the ever-present threat that it might claim her? And how, given all the baseball books and magazines I've consumed through the years, could that erroneous notion persist? I'm ashamed and won't be surprised should bat-wielding thugs from the Society for American Baseball Research confront me in the staircase and confiscate my membership card.

"The whole history of baseball has the quality of mythology," said Bernard Malamud, author of *The Natural*.

The Babe not an orphan? Say it ain't so.

One display, set against a royal red background, features Ty Cobb. It includes his late-career A's jersey with elephant emblem, an oatmeal-colored sweater from his Detroit days, and the ornate George "Honey Boy" Evans trophy, once bestowed annually upon the game's best hitter. Small photos show Ty evading a tag, awaiting a pitch, and gloving a ball. One large portrait dominates the case, of Cobb with his Grandma Muse smile, serious eyes piercing the distance. It sets the tone and reinforces what we all think we know about Ty Cobb—that he was the toughest, fiercest, meanest SOB in all of baseball, that he could deliver pain and endure it in equal measures. But then, beneath the photo, you notice something out of place, something that softens his harsh image. A set of sliding pads. Ty Cobb wore sliding pads? Pads of cushy, comfortable lamb's wool, the kind upon which a mother might lay a bare-bottomed baby. Think of the years you played ball yourself, perfecting your slide on gravelly fields that rubbed like a rake and left bloody raspberries on your thigh, calf, and bum. "Slide right and that won't happen," your coach said. You endured it because you knew that's how the pros did it. Probably Kaline and Rose. Certainly Cobb. No one ever told you about sliding pads.

My dad played sports—baseball, football, hockey—year-round with a crew of scrappy neighborhood kids. It was the Depression and for equipment they used whatever they could scrounge. You might see them on ice armed with homemade hockey sticks, their bodies protected by football pads, a catcher's shin guards, or even pieces of cardboard strapped to their legs. But never sliding pads for baseball.

"Hmm," Dad says. "I never used them. But I didn't slide that much. Cobb liked to slide."

We wander through the early decades of the game and admire the relics.

Kid Nichols's gold watch.

Cy Young's scrapbook.

Christy Mathewson's faded red socks, which elicit a chuckle.

"What?" Joey asks.

When Jeff Mancini and I were boys convinced that the Hall of Fame would come calling, we agreed to save mementoes of our early playing days, figuring they would be in demand by museums and at charity auctions. I don't know how long he kept it up, but by the time my career had concluded I had a drawer full of stirrups with elastic that no longer snapped and a mess of tangled athletic supporters. (I had heard that some sports stars got their jock straps bronzed.) My mom suspected a fetish.

Honus Wagner's uniform.

Babe Ruth's blue-marble Ebonite bowling ball.

Joe Jackson's shoes. Most fans know at least two things about "Shoeless" Joe: first, that he hit brilliantly; second, that baseball disowned him. The latter keeps him out of the Hall of Fame but not the museum. Though you won't find Jackson in the Hall's solemn gallery of plaques, you will find him—as well as Pete Rose and other vanquished souls—in the exhibits that tell the story of the game, a story that would be glaringly incomplete without mention of the Black Sox Scandal and Rose's record 4,256 hits.

Frankie Frisch's cap.

Joe Medwick's jersey.

A Dizzy Dean button.

We are amid St. Louis's Gas House Gang, a team that Detroiters Dad's age recall with derision for derailing the city's 1934 World Series hopes, a cast of oddballs known by their nicknames. Dizzy, Daffy, Ducky, and Pepper. And on the wall across from them is . . .

Charlie Gehringer's bronzed glove.

It gives you a sense of the passing of time to stand beside your father, who is in his ninth decade, as he studies the mitt of the man he has admired since the days of Herbert Hoover. Discovered by outfielder Bobby Veach in 1923, farm boy Charlie Gehringer got a tryout with Detroit late in the season and impressed player-manager Ty Cobb. He signed for a $300 bonus and headed to the minor leagues the next spring.

Gehringer lived on a farm in rural Fowlerville with his German-born parents, two sisters, and an older brother. They planted corn, oats, and barley and raised dairy cows. "My brother, being five years older, ran all the machinery, so my mother and sisters and I had to do the tedious jobs," said Gehringer. "It seemed I had all the hard jobs—the weeding, shocking up the wheat, digging potatoes—mostly the hand work. Milking cows was the hardest."

His brother wanted to be a farmer. Charlie didn't.

On Sundays Charlie played ball near the Gehringer barn in a pasture that had been mowed into the shape of a diamond. For bases he filled grain sacks with sand. "My mother heartily disapproved," he said. "She thought baseball was a waste of time."

That would change.

In 1924 Gehringer's father died, never having seen his son play professionally. Gehringer left his London, Ontario, team and came home for the funeral. He was docked three days' pay.

"Good old Charlie Gehringer," Dad says, and he needn't say anything more. I can fill the blanks with a childhood worth of stories about Dad's truest, most enduring, second-to-none baseball hero.

How Charlie never swung at the first pitch, spotting his opponent that strike.

How he never bragged, letting his talents speak for him.

How he grew up in Michigan, played only for the Tigers, and stayed in our city.

How he cared for his widowed mother, remaining a bachelor until she died.

Even Grandma Stankiewicz, who disliked baseball and the scoundrels she assumed practiced it, approved of Charlie Gehringer. Like Grandma, he was a good Catholic, faithful to his church, faithful to God.

Charlie Gehringer's life became an allegory, its lessons implicit. Be patient. Be humble. Be loyal and loving and devoted. Above all, care for your mother. Come to think of it, that's pretty much how my dad has lived his own life.

Look back at the local papers from that time period, in the days before television dethroned the press as the premier visual medium. In addition to the photos of Charlie and his teammates framed in circles or clumped in montages, in addition to the stories describing him as a mechanical man, a silent knight, a modest hero, a gentleman, or a gliding gray ghost of the infield, you will find features about Charlie and Mrs. Gehringer.

"He lives with his mother at 14505 Woodmont, a new stone residence he bought for her recently," one reporter wrote. "It is only a short walk to St. Mary's Catholic Church, where Gehringer and his mother are regular and active members of the parish."

You will come upon pictures of Mrs. Gehringer listening to an away game beside the radio, her gray hair lifted into a bun, or of her at the ballpark in a front-row seat and flowered hat with a corsage on her lapel.

You will see her quoted in the paper. "This has been a grand town for Charlie," she said. "I just know from what he tells me he would quit the game before he even would try baseball anywhere else."

After she's gone and after his playing days have ended, you will find headlines that proclaim, "Gehringer Weds Secretary." To avoid the attention that would have accompanied a hometown wedding, Gehringer drove to the West Coast to be married in California in June 1949, and consequently he missed the hanging of his plaque in Cooperstown.

When Gehringer died at age eighty-nine, Shirley Povich of the *Washington Post* lamented the lack of attention his passing brought. "Among the most deprived of the nation's baseball fans were those born too late to see Charlie Gehringer play second base," he wrote. "Charlie Gehringer didn't know how to strut. He was . . . baseball's quiet man, content to let his . . . glove speak for him."

All these many seasons later, its bronzed fingers spread open, it still does.

CHARLIE GEHRINGER
19 YEARS. 8,860 AT BATS. 2,839 HITS.
1,774 RUNS SCORED. .320 AVERAGE.

11. July 1972:
Willie in the Dugout

Two days before the All-Star Game, with his Tigers in first place, Billy Martin sent a telegram to Earl Weaver demanding that he not use Mickey Lolich more than two innings in the Midsummer Classic.

"If he pitches more than that, it will hurt our whole rotation and our pennant chances," Martin told reporters. "Let Weaver pitch some of his twenty-game winners."

Weaver did. He chose his ace, Jim Palmer, to start for the American League. Lolich, who was leading the majors with 17 wins, followed in the fourth and fifth innings, combining with Palmer to shut out the National League until Henry Aaron thrilled the hometown crowd with a two-run smash in the

ABOVE: Willie Horton *(Detroit Public Library, Burton Historical Collection)*

sixth off Gaylord Perry. The National League won 4-3 in ten innings.

But Billy Martin was focused on the East Division race with the Orioles. He tried to give a positive spin to the fact that Al Kaline was injured and that Willie Horton, who had slugged 22 home runs the year prior, was slumping. "I would say Mr. Weaver is in trouble," said Martin. "When we start hitting, Baltimore is really going to be in trouble and we are due. . . . He's going to have a hell of a time beating us when we are healthy."

On Tuesdays when new magazines arrived at Sterling Drugs, I walked to the pharmacy, darting across five lanes of 13 Mile Road, past the barbershop where I got haircuts—"Boy's regular, please"—around the corner from Little Caesar's Pizza, to peruse the latest edition of the *Sporting News,* ignoring the NO LOITERING sign taped to the shelf, hoping the clerk with the silver beehive hairdo wouldn't shoo me away while I scanned the minor-league numbers for Toledo Mudhens who might be on the road to Detroit.

Once a month a fresh issue of *Baseball Digest* tempted with headlines punctuated with exclamation points and question marks:

"Willie Davis, Man on the Move!"

"Relief Pitchers: Specialists in Crisis!"

"Denny McLain: Comeback or Washout?"

"Reggie Jackson: This Will Be His Year!"

Inside on newsprint were a roster of stories, a "quick quiz," a crossword puzzle, a feature where a star recalled "the game I'll never forget," and a column by Lou Boudreau offering tips for "budding ball players." Kids wrote in and asked how to strengthen their pitching arms or what size bat Lou thought they should use.

"The name of the game is contact," Lou said.

We took advice wherever we could find it: from fathers and uncles and brothers, from Boston catcher Duane Josephson on the back of milk cartons, from the 16mm films that St. Malachy manager Ray Szydlak showed in his basement, from the instructional TV shows that ran early Saturday mornings, and from Pee Wee Reese.

Reese offered his wisdom to young hitters in the *1972 Famous Slugger Yearbook*, a slender volume put out annually by bat-maker Hillerich & Bradsby. It featured Bill Melton, Tony Oliva, and Willie Stargell on the cover and included tips on caring for your bat, descriptions of the autograph models ("Johnny Bench, small barrel tapers gradually into small size handle with medium size knob"), and team photos of youth-league and college championship squads from around the country. One of the teams came from Detroit, the Kowalski Sausage Baseball Federation Sophomore Champions. I didn't recognize any of the names: "Dave Ling, Randy Owen, Dale Petroskey . . ."

"You should use a bat you can handle comfortably," Pee Wee recommended.

It was the same boring advice every adult gave, and it countered the inclination of most kids to grab the longest, heaviest, biggest-barreled monster of a club they could manage.

Equipment made the ball player. You wanted your own bat. But other things helped establish you as a serious player: spikes instead of tennis shoes, a batting glove, terry-cloth wristbands to absorb the sweat, a weighted doughnut to use in the on-deck circle, a first baseman's mitt just in case, a rosin bag to enhance your pitching grip, a swipe of "black-eye" above your cheeks to mute the sun's reflection and give you that professional look. Some kids even owned catcher's gear.

But nothing was more personal than your glove. Every kid who played had one. A bat could break. But a glove lasted, even if you left it in the rain, and it went with you, hanging from the handlebar of your bike, resting on your bedroom dresser while you slept.

When I began organized baseball, Dad replaced my blue Kmart mitt with a Wilson glove. I chose the Willie Horton Pro Style.

"That's a nigger glove," said Marty, one of my teammates.

In our neighborhood there was one black person, Bobby Burda's adopted brother, and he lived five or six streets over. Everyone else was white. Racism tinted our lives, not the violent Klan variety but something more subtle. It was there in things big and small, in how our school had a moment of silence for Robert Kennedy but not for Martin Luther King Jr., in the words we used to taunt each other, in the way most kids rooted for whatever boxer might be facing Muhammad Ali.

Many who relocated to Warren and other suburbs of the '50s and '60s moved from Detroit as their streets integrated. Some blamed blacks for the city's crime and deterioration, and sought refuge in segregated communities. The 1967 race riots sharpened the divide.

Through much of the 1970s, my Uncle Teddy lived in the Detroit house where he, my dad, and their siblings were raised. He had bars on his windows and talked a lot about "getting out" because of break-ins on his block.

"I know how to solve that," said one of my friend's fathers. "You get a shotgun and you sit in the dark at night and you wait for them coons to come through that door and you blast them. That's all they understand."

For a lot of us white kids in our part of the world, Willie Horton was the first black person we felt we really knew. He grew up in Detroit, played on the city's sandlot fields, and became a Tiger at twenty, recording his first 100-RBI season two years later. When Detroit won the championship, Horton hit 36 home runs, second in the league only to Frank Howard, and he gunned down Lou Brock in the crucial fifth game of the World Series. An All-Star several times and always among the team leaders in home runs, he bulged with power.

While Al Kaline brought quiet brilliance and calm consistency to the field, Horton brought heart and force and feeling. He could be moody. (He once walked out on the team for several days and another time announced his retirement in anger over treatment by Billy Martin.) Horton showed his emotions—his hurt over criticism, his ferocity during brawls—and in doing so captured the loyalty of a legion of young fans.

Before July 16 he had already won my devotion. But at a game that day, he assured it would never waver.

Uncle Teddy, a Chrysler union steward, had landed four last-minute tickets and asked Dad, me, and my sister, Colleen, to go with him.

No place on Earth brought me more thrills during childhood than Tiger Stadium. It opened on the same day as Boston's Fenway Park in 1912, several years after my Polish grandfather

Theodore Stankiewicz immigrated to America. It was called Navin Field then, and my grandpa set out to learn about baseball there and at semipro fields around Detroit. He came to love America's pastime, taking the streetcar to Michigan and Trumbull to see Ty Cobb, Sam Crawford, and Bobby Veach, the era's best outfield. In time, he took his six sons, including Dad and Uncle Teddy, and they watched Harry Heilmann and Hank Greenberg and Gehrig and DiMaggio and Williams and so many others. Dad introduced Joey and me to the sport in that same cement-and-steel structure.

We arrived a half hour before Sunday's game and parked the Nova in Corktown in the yard of a woman whose smile had gaps where teeth used to be. Along Trumbull Avenue, street characters sold home-packed peanuts and oddly shaped, candy-striped balloons. Uncle Teddy led us past them, through the gate and turnstiles beyond the players' parking lot and into the shadowy concourse that ran beneath the stands. A cacophony of voices—exuberant children, loud, beer-drinking men, vendors hawking dogs and programs—enveloped us. We marched up the same ramps that my dad and uncle had traveled since boyhood. My uncle took us through a narrow, caged catwalk toward the streaming sunlight at the other end. We emerged near our upper-deck box seats, their wooden frames a glossy green, a few shades darker than the grass.

The Tiger dugout was directly below, and when Detroit came to bat in the last of the first, Horton was sitting outside the dugout on the steps at the far end, thirty feet beneath me.

"Willll-lieee!" I yelled down. "Willll-lieee!"

But he didn't respond.

The stadium looked pretty much as it did in 1938 when Dad turned eighteen. The stands had been double-decked that year, giving the park an overhang in right field. The place felt intimate, hugged by 50,000 seats, some closer to home plate than the shortstop.

Uncle Teddy loved baseball as much as I did. At age fifty-six, four years older than my dad, he played fast-pitch softball in leagues dominated by men half his age. Perched on the edge of his seat, he scanned the ball field, his big grin punctuated by two pronounced, Red Skelton dimples.

Of my favorite Tigers—Kaline, Lolich, and Horton—only Willie played that afternoon. He was in left field. Rookie pitcher Bill Slayback, who had debuted weeks earlier with seven no-hit innings, faced a Kansas City Royals team that included the league's top hitters, Richie Scheinblum, Lou Piniella, and Amos Otis, all of whom had slipped past Joe Rudi and ahead of Boston rookie Carlton Fisk in the race for the batting title. Slayback cruised through the early innings untouched, and the Tigers got off to a quick lead when Norm Cash launched a solo shot to right field, his 17th home run, two shy of Richie Allen.

We stood and cheered as Cash crossed the plate. Horton and Mickey Stanley greeted him. Uncle Teddy shaded a diamond on his scoresheet.

Unlike my father, Uncle Teddy did not temper his emotions, particularly when it came to baseball, a sport he felt he knew better than most paid managers. He regularly challenged their decisions.

"Ted's a lousy poker player," Dad often said. "He can't hide his feelings."

In the fourth inning Jim Northrup got nailed trying to steal home.

My uncle yelped. "Oh-ah-geez. What's Martin doing? Northrup can't run. He's slow."

Uncle Teddy darted his head from my dad to me, as if looking for support. His face was red, his voice high-pitched, and his clipped Polish accent noticeable, filling his sentences with errant soft "ah" sounds.

"What? Does he think he's-ah Ty-ah Cobb? He can't even-ah steal second. Why's he-ah trying home?"

He looked over the railing, toward the dugout and Billy Martin.

"What's he thinking?" he said. "You just cost us a run, Billy."

A half inning later when the Royals loaded the bases with two outs, Uncle Teddy added, "Ah, here we go," as if the baseball gods would soon punish us for Northrup's foolishness.

But Cookie Rojas lined to Horton for the final out.

"We got-ah lucky there."

In the lull of the middle innings Dad and Uncle Teddy got talking about ball players, names I had come to know well: Charlie Gehringer, of course; Hal Newhouser, Dad's sandlot rival; little Tommy Bridges, my grandfather's favorite; and Hank Greenberg, who might have hit 500 home runs had he not been called to serve during World War II like so many stars of the time and like my father, Uncle Teddy, and most of their brothers. Some of the Stankiewicz men went overseas and fought on the front lines. All came home alive, Uncle Bucky earning a Purple Heart after being hit by shrapnel in Africa.

I didn't know many major leaguers who had fought in Vietnam. The Tiger yearbook had photos of pitcher Mike Kilkenny visiting troops for the USO. Kilkenny, who had been traded in May, wore a flak jacket and helmet in the picture. But none of the current players' career records showed gaps of three or four years like *The Baseball Encyclopedia* entries for Greenberg, The Great Ted Williams, and Bob Feller.

"Don't the players have to go to Vietnam, too?" I asked.

"They're mainly in the-ah reserves," said Uncle Teddy. "Old Lolich was in the reserves. . . . They do their time off-season. It's not like in our-ah day, right Joe? Not like in the-ah olden days."

"The olden days?" said Dad, chuckling. "They ain't that old."

After hot dogs and sodas and several hands of unshelled peanuts, Dad took Colleen to the restroom. She was too young to wander by herself.

I stayed with my uncle. Though married, he had no kids of his own but he served as godfather to several of us.

"Uncle Teddy, did you ever go to the Hall of Fame?"

He frowned and shook his head.

"Me and Dad might go there this year."

"How's-ah that?"

"Why?"

"Well, your pa says your ma's going back into the hospital real soon. And when do you-ah start school?"

"I dunno."

Uncle Teddy lifted his Tigers cap off his head, stroked his hairless skull, and then arched his eyebrows.

"You think Willie Horton will get in?" I asked.

"Un-unh. He's a cry-ah-baby."

I spent much of the game with my head resting on the guardrail, looking down at the dugout, trying to draw Willie's attention, trying to bridge the distance between us, trying to somehow show him that I was different from all of the other boys, that I was a real fan, one who would be going to Cooperstown. How I convinced myself of that after all the evidence to the contrary perplexes me now. But I believed it. Regardless of Uncle Teddy's doubts, I knew my dad would be taking me to Cooperstown.

Whenever Detroit came to bat and Willie Horton sat partly outside the dugout, I called his name in the singsongy manner that kids once used.

"Willll-lieee! Willll-lieee!"

Finally, in the eighth inning, Horton glanced up, looked my way, paused as if measuring my intentions, and then raised his right hand toward me like a third base coach halting a runner.

For a while the world seemed a perfect place.

12. Tommie's Big Brother

*Perhaps he didn't have the greatest fastball in
    the league.*
*His curveball didn't break real sharp, his change
    held no intrigue.*
*The reason why he holds a Cy Young trophy in
    both hands*
*Is Gaylord Perry's Hall of Famer salivary
    glands.*

—Mark W. Schraf's poem "Gaylord"
from *Cooperstown Verses*

It used to be a decent baseball trivia question. Which brothers hit the most major-league home runs? In the early 1970s, if you asked an old-timer he would search his memory for siblings who had each attained a measure of success, like the slugging version of the Perry pitchers, Gaylord and Jim. He'd consider the Boyers, the Waners, the Alous, maybe the Walkers.

"The DiMaggios," he might finally answer.

"Wrong," you'd say. "The Aarons, Hank and Tommie."

It almost qualified as a trick question because Hank hit gobs of home runs and Tommie managed just thirteen.

"Oh, that's a good one."

The nugget of trivia came at Tommie Aaron's expense, reducing him to a punch line—as if he didn't already have enough to deal with being five-and-a-half years younger than Hank, following him up through high school and into the minor leagues.

Any kid who felt swallowed by his brother's shadow had to have a measure of compassion for the younger Aaron. Not only did he try to make it in the same sport, he played on the same teams, the Braves in Milwaukee and Atlanta, and sometimes at the same positions. He couldn't escape the comparisons. Their stats ran one after another in *The Baseball Encyclopedia* on the opening page of the register, Hank coming before Tommie in the alphabet, too. Even the headlines that ran above his photos in the scant stories that might have been pasted in his slender scrapbook alluded to Henry:

"Another Aaron."

"Managing to Set a Mark All His Own."

"Tommie Aaron: Only 702 Home Runs to Go."

Hecklers never let him forget. When he hit a home run, a fan might yell that Hank had hit two that day. "You can't compare Henry and me," he said once. "No two men are alike and nobody understands that more than me."

Almost every lengthy story about Tommie Aaron included comments from Hank, who played the role of big brother admirably, deflecting some of the spotlight off himself and onto his sibling. "Tommie never had the opportunity to prove what he could do," he said. "The Braves never played him enough. I know he could have been a very good ball player."

Relationships between brothers can be complex things.

Our backyard on Shawn Drive bordered the backyard of a family of four boys close in age. The two oldest, Greg and Gary, struggled continually for supremacy. They ridiculed one another with vengefulness, Gary often challenging the age-dictated hierarchy that had placed Greg at the front of the line. I once saw Gary peg his brother with an ice ball that he had stored in the freezer months earlier for that specific purpose. The cruelty they inflicted upon one another could only be equaled in intensity by their unity when threatened by one outside the family.

I used to be envious of Greg and Gary and the Mancinis and the Metts down the street and other families where the brothers were so close in age that they could be best friends if they chose. They had what Joey and I didn't—and don't.

I think of Tommie Aaron when entering Hank's room at the museum, my own brother near me. Many years have passed since I felt the weight of Joey's achievements. But there was a time when teachers and neighbors measured me against his successes. My parents hung his artwork on the living room wall, along with the ribbons he had won at the state fair. "You should take up art like Joey," an uncle once suggested. It was the last thing I wanted to do.

Dad took me to Joey's football games at Melby Junior High, and I witnessed from the bleachers as he broke tackles and spun for touchdowns. Parents whooped and hollered, his teammates gave him skin, and cheerleaders swirled in blue and gray. After the game I carried his helmet to the car, walking beside him, he was bigger than usual in shoulder pads.

No matter how old you get, you never entirely escape your childhood relationships. They mold your life and affect you in ways that you don't always see.

In the public eye Tommie Aaron never emerged from his brother's shadow. His last headline came in 1984 in *Jet* magazine when he succumbed to leukemia at age forty-five. It said, "Hank's Brother Tommie Dies."

Hank Aaron's room shares a wall with Babe Ruth's room but they feel worlds apart. The light in Aaron's room seems brighter, the shadows harder, the display antiseptic, like a hospital. By contrast Ruth's room feels washed in wonder, a classic movie house. Some of the difference is actual and tangible, some a matter of perception. Like most adults who visit the museum, I remember Aaron and his pursuit of Ruth's home-run record. It wasn't that long ago in the breadth of a full life. But Ruth's playing days are far removed, his last game coming sixty-six years ago in the throes of the Depression and before the dawn of World War II. Today, memories of him as a hitter exist only in the minds of those in their seventies and older.

Babe Ruth's camel-colored polo coat hangs in a display case among items from the Barry Halper Collection in another room, where exhibits change regularly. It's a long coat, reaching to Ruth's knees. You can probably picture him in it.

"Yep, that's his," Dad says. "He wore that coat all the time."

My dad saw Ruth at Navin Field in the 1930s. But he no longer remembers any of the specifics, just a varnished, time-worn sense of having been there in Ruth's huge presence. I can imagine Dad at the ballpark with brothers and buddies, a motley collection of working-class kids like the Our Gang bunch, only older and tougher, with cracking and changed voices. They would have walked the six or seven miles from their neighborhood, saving the streetcar fare for a hot dog or a box of Cracker

Jack. They'd be in the cheap seats out in right field before the park had a second deck, and they'd be calling out to Pete Fox or Jo-Jo White or Gee Walker, whoever was stationed in center and right for the Tigers, and cheering wildly for Ruth when he lumbered onto the field. I imagine The Bambino tipping his hat to the boys in the stands, maybe razzing with them from a distance or tossing a ball into the seats, that inextinguishable cheerfulness on his ruddy face.

Throughout America for most of eighty years, any child drawn to baseball has learned two names when exploring the history of the sport: Babe Ruth and Ty Cobb, the game's greatest players. For those of us who grew up Tiger fans, we also learned that Cobb was the better of the two, a "genius in spikes" it says on his plaque at the old park. But even given our hometown bias, we realized that Ruth was an almost universal hero of Paul Bunyanesque size, perhaps surpassed by Cobb in talent but far above him and all others in legend.

Though forty years separate my father's childhood from mine, as boys we both read books about Ruth and dreamed of such success and pretended to be him on the ball field and measured our other heroes' achievements against his. When we see Ruth in the museum now, we see him yet through those same eyes. We know of his faults but he remains a glossy figure.

It's different with Hank Aaron. When I see the video of Aaron's 715th home run, with him rounding the bases and nudging away a pair of fans attempting to merge with his historic trot, I remember the derision and the controversy that followed him for two seasons. I remember how, as with Roger Maris earlier, many hated to see Ruth's record fall. I remember the stories of the threatening letters Aaron received, the racism that surfaced during his home-run chase, the relief he said he felt when it was all over.

Such stark realities existed in Ruth's era, too, but they're diffused by time and memory, and my dad has never talked much of them.

The museum's major exhibit moves chronologically through the game's history. There are the earliest years—of the Boston Beaneaters, for example—that predate all of our memories, including the ones Dad's father passed to him. Then there's Grandpa's days of Cobb, Crawford, and Walter Johnson. Then Dad begins recalling the players he saw: Gehrig, Jimmie Foxx, DiMaggio, Feller; and then my brother: Mantle and Musial and Whitey Ford; and then me.

Earl Weaver's Orioles. The Miracle Mets. The Pirates of Roberto Clemente. Sparky and the Big Red Machine. The Oakland A's dynasty.

I remember thinking as a boy how foolish Vida Blue was to reject Charlie Finley's name-change offer of $2,000. Finley wanted Vida to adopt "True" as part of his name, as in "True" Blue, to complement fellow pitchers "Catfish" Hunter and "Blue Moon" Odom. Vida refused.

"What a dummy," Jeff Mancini said.

I agreed. "He's an idiot. I'd change my name for a thousand dollars."

"Me too," said Jeff.

Much later I grew to appreciate Vida Blue for standing up

to Finley. His explanation made the difference. "Vida was my father's name," he said. "It's the Spanish word for life. Now that he's dead I honor him every time the name Vida Blue appears in the headlines."

My brother is steps ahead of me, reading about Thurman Munson, Sparky Lyle, and the rest of Billy Martin's Yankees.

"You remember Reggie's home run?" he asks.

How could I not? It took flight on a windy Tuesday evening in mid-July of 1971. The All-Star contest had come to Tiger Stadium, and all of the game's biggest names graced the field. In the third inning, with Luis Aparicio on base, Reggie smashed a Dock Ellis pitch an estimated 520 feet into the lighting structure on the roof in right-center. Al Kaline said he had never seen a ball hit harder. It looked as if it was still rising when it struck.

"Yeah, I remember Reggie's home run."

My brother had joined Dad and me in the living room to watch the game on television. I was ten, he was seventeen, and I tried mightily to impress him.

"Can you believe Earl Weaver's starting Vida Blue instead of Mickey Lolich?" And so began a two-hour monologue incorporating everything I knew or thought I knew about baseball, mostly facts drawn from the backs of Topps cards and the colorful metallic coins that accompanied them in 1971.

"Did you know that Mike Cuellar's from Cuba? . . . Did you know that the National League has won eight straight All-Star Games? . . . Hey, Joey, you should like Johnny Bench because he's part Indian. . . . Rod Carew stole home seven times in 1969. . . . Babe Ruth was an orphan. . . . Carl Yastrzemski won the Triple Crown in 1967—no, not the horse races, Joey. Ha, that's funny. It's where you lead the league in home runs, RBIs, and batting average. . . . Willie Stargell hit the first home run ever at Shea Stadium, bet you didn't know that? . . . When Johnny Bench was a kid he could have died in a bus accident like some of his teammates. . . . Al Kaline's dad was a broom-maker—that sounds weird, doesn't it? . . . I don't think Lou Brock will pass Ty Cobb, do you? . . . Did you know Ty Cobb's son had a brain tumor? But his was worse 'cause he died. . . . Mickey Lolich grew up in Oregon. . . . Frank Robinson has hit a home run in every major-league park. . . . Wow! That home run could put Reggie Jackson in the Hall of Fame."

I told them everything that came to mind—except for one thing. Bobby Murcer played center for the Yankees. Early in his career some thought he might be as good as Mickey Mantle. But before he became a starter, Murcer had been a soldier in the Vietnam War. When he came to the plate in the All-Star Game, I didn't mention that fact, not wanting to spoil the moment.

Just months earlier Joey had been marching against the conflict.

He, Jim O'Connor, and their friends skipped school on the last Friday in April, joining 2,500 protestors in a mile-and-a-half hike from the community college in Warren. They trampled over the lawns of surprised suburbanites and on to Van Dyke Avenue with arms linked and down the street toward the tank plant, "a symbol of the white racist machine that is destroying this country," according to leaflets. The same tank plant where Dad worked. Some carried upside down American flags and signs urging PEACE and demanding ALL TROOPS OUT OF INDO-

CHINA. Some chanted, "One, two, three, four, we don't want your fucking war." Others yelled, "Nixon, pull out early like your father should have."

"Traitors," cried a small group of counterdemonstrators as the protestors passed. Riot police kept the two sides apart, and a military helicopter hovered above the avenue.

The marchers roared past the tank plant's main gate. Somewhere among the crowd of students in jeans and army jackets was my brother, and somewhere inside the gate was my father. His job that day was to take pictures of the students in case violence broke out. You can guess who didn't appear on Dad's negatives.

"Do you remember," I ask my brother now, "how the year after Reggie's home run, in 1972, all I could talk about was coming here to Cooperstown?"

"No, not really," he says.

"How could you not remember?"

"Well, I'm sure you probably wanted to come. I just don't recall it."

"Your memory's really going, old man."

"Baseball—that's all you ever talked about," he says. "Everything was about baseball for you."

He's right, and I feel good that he remembers that. Being amid the nearly life-size cutouts of "Catfish" Hunter and Tom Seaver and the shots of Sparky Lyle and Brooks Robinson and the gloves of Morgan and Bench and the mementoes of all those other guys whose careers crossed into 1972 summons a time when not much in life rated higher than the sport.

Baseball captivated me and enchanted me and to a large degree defined me. The biggest questions I pondered weren't about Vietnam or Watergate or the ones posed by the sixth-grade curriculum. They were about baseball. Will Mickey Lolich win thirty games? How many balls can Johnny Bench hold in his hand? Will Mr. Szydlak let me pitch?

Junior high school provides a stark contrast between students. Some who mature early appear on the edge of adulthood. Others seem trapped in fourth-grade bodies. I saw the differences in Miss Itkin's social studies room. Doug, a kid in too-short jeans, liked to paint a layer of rubber cement on his desk and roll it into a dirty little ball. Debbie often taunted Julie, who wore Donny Osmond T-shirts and didn't know why the Rolling Stones had named their album *Sticky Fingers*. Some kids spread rumors of spider eggs in Bubble Yum. Others told where to buy weed. A few of us immersed ourselves in baseball. And nothing really compared.

Almost three dozen men who took the field in 1972 have made it into the Hall of Fame or will soon (in Mazeroski's case). Not all shone that season. Hoyt Wilhelm faded away at forty-nine, saving a single game. Aparicio stole only three bases, Cepeda knocked in a miserable nine runs, McCovey hit for a lowly .213, and Marichal endured his first losing campaign—a dandy one at that, 6–16.

It was a season of emerging Carltons: Fisk as an All-Star in Boston, Steve atop the leader boards in Philadelphia. For Brooks, there was another Gold Glove; for Stargell, another hundred ribbies. Bench led in home runs, Brock in stolen bases, and Billy Williams in average. Joe Morgan walked and scored more than anyone, Rod Carew captured another AL batting title, and Nolan Ryan got his first strikeout crown. Niekro, Gibson, and Yaz were merely ordinary, but Palmer, Perry, Hunter, and Seaver won twenty yet again. Fergie did it a sixth straight time and Sutton with his nine shutouts fell one short. Rollie and Reggie got their first World Series rings, Sparky and Perez didn't. Old Frank Robinson went West and Old Willie Mays went East and Earl's Orioles stayed home—finally. Kaline and Killebrew reached familiar feats—.300-plus for Al, 25 homers for Harmon—that would elude them in their remaining years. And Hank Aaron pulled to within 41 of Babe Ruth.

That autumn also brought rookie Mike Schmidt's first hit and Roberto Clemente's 3,000th and last (in the regular season, anyway).

It's somewhere after that in the museum, after the displays with Reggie and Vida Blue and Johnny Bench, when the warm fuzziness of nostalgia dissipates, when the players pictured no longer trace their beginnings back to my childhood. Here the tone changes, in my heart at least.

13. Baseball Pilgrims

Bobby Doerr first appeared on a Hall of Fame ballot in 1953. Thirty-three years later, with the support of teammate Ted Williams, the former Boston second baseman made it into the shrine. For the induction that summer, Doerr took a road trip of his own, driving a van from California with his ninety-three-year-old mother and other family members.

It's dark when we leave the museum, emerging along Main Street into the night air and onto sidewalks tinged with the light of street lamps. We aren't alone. Couples and families and other collections of fathers, mothers, sons, daughters, and friends stroll to restaurants and hotels, pointing out collectibles in store windows, absorbing the soothing spirit of the town.

"How about an ice cream?" Dad asks.

And now I really feel like a kid, a forty-year-old kid whose Dad just offered him ice cream. It makes me laugh.

I loved to hear that question as a boy. He always sprang it unexpectedly. Though some treats became routine—cheesy pizzas from the Tender Touch bar on Saturday evenings, jelly doughnuts on Sunday mornings while scouring the long list of players' averages in the bloated sports section—the ice cream trips came as surprises, like shortstop home runs.

The Red Nugget parlor is around the corner from the bookstore, beyond the Bullpen bagel shop. Ceiling fans struggle to cool the place, which is decorated with replicas of vintage Coca-Cola advertisements. Britney Spears moans on the radio as two teenagers work the counter, scooping mint chip and butter pecan for a line of customers.

A rumpled man follows us up the wooden steps. The screen door slaps closed behind him. He stops and considers the clump of people before him, muttering as he begrudgingly falls in behind us.

"Lot of people in town," I say, judging him a local.

He nods.

"Must be a pretty exciting time around here."

"Yeah," he says. "No parking. Lines for ice cream. . . . My favorite part's on Monday—when everybody leaves."

"Oh, I didn't think about that." I turn to my brother, assuming our exchange has ended. But the stranger, perhaps regretting his tone or suspecting me a chamber of commerce spy, adds a few friendlier words. "But this is Cooperstown, and every fan worth his salt has to make a pilgrimage to Cooperstown."

Baseball as religion—it qualifies as cliché. But you cannot escape it. It flows through the sport, through its language, literature, and legend.

We call our ballparks Green Cathedrals. We refer to the Hall of Fame as The Shrine. We worship our idols, swear devotion to our teams, and elevate our heroes to something that borders sainthood by immortalizing the best of them and excluding those fallen angels—Pete Rose, Joe Jackson, Ed Cicotte—who, though talented enough, sin against the sport.

Perhaps it started with the Knickerbockers of the 1840s who played their games at Elysian Fields, named for the mythological place to which good souls ascend after death. But the connection grew deeper, to the point where Ray Kinsella in *Shoeless Joe* hears a voice—God as a baseball announcer?—urging him to build a park for the spirits of passed players. Then there's Annie Savoy in *Bull Durham*: "I've tried 'em all, I really have, and the only church that truly feeds the soul is the Church of Baseball."

The association is not lost on those who run the Hall of Fame. When the gallery expanded in the 1990s, architects gave the addition a dome to enhance the sense of sacredness. Its leaders have taken to calling the museum "the spiritual home of baseball."

And, yes, people make pilgrimages.

Harold Gach came in May 2000 on Memorial Day weekend. Someone watching as he hobbled toward the entrance on that warm afternoon might have wondered what stopped him on the steps with his wife Shelley beside him and his friends Allan and Rhona Anchill in front.

The Anchills had invited the Gachs to Cooperstown. Harold and Allan had been friends since the 1960s. They played ball on the same teams, hung out with the same crowd, went to major-league games together, rooted for Kaline and Mantle. Over time, as other high school friendships faded, theirs grew stronger. Harold was an only child, and he and Allan were like brothers. They took trips; they stood up at each other's weddings. When Allan became a dad, he called Harold first. When Harold had a son, he asked Allan to be godfather. There were parties, vacations, a bar mitzvah, and baseball—thirty-five years' worth before the cancer surfaced.

Until their journey to Cooperstown, Allan did not realize the degree to which the illness had ravaged his friend. A big man at six-two, Harold had lost sixty pounds. He had become so thin that when he grabbed two complimentary apples from a hotel counter and put one in each of his pockets the weight was enough to drop his pants to his ankles as he walked through the lobby. He hadn't lost his sense of humor, though. He laughed about the apples.

Harold looked gaunt and yellow with jaundice. He staggered when he stepped. He tired quickly when he drove. His wife and friends recognized what they thought Harold did not: that his life was coming to an end.

In the previous year he and Shelley had been to Maui and Paradise Island. He loved to travel. There were baseball trips to see the Mudhens in Toledo, the Reds in Cincinnati, the Indians in Cleveland. To Wrigley Field to admire his son David's favorite, Andre Dawson. To St. Louis and Kansas City by van. To Pittsburgh. To the five parks in California. Some with the whole family: Shelley, David, daughter Caryn; others with just David. Twenty-two parks in all.

The sport connected father and son. For six years they ran a part-time memorabilia business, David's and Dad's Sports Cards and Collectibles, as much for pleasure as profit. They took their enterprise on the road, doing shows during the day and visiting ballparks at night. David played the game from T-ball through high school, Harold never far from the field. David even considered pursuing a career as an umpire.

The two of them had been talking for a long time about going to Cooperstown. First, they had wanted to visit all the ballparks but new ones were being built too rapidly. "I had always hoped that Cooperstown would be the culmination of our baseball endeavors together," said David.

The cancer came suddenly late in the summer of 1999 after Harold's fiftieth birthday. By the next spring it had entered its final stage. Though Harold refused to concede to it, he set short-term goals. He wanted to watch his son graduate from college in May, he wanted to visit the Hall of Fame, and he wanted to see a friend's son pass the bar. He fulfilled the first two.

After graduating from Michigan State University, David and a friend toured the Middle East and Europe. He was overseas when his parents and their friends the Anchills went to William Cooper's village beside Otsego Lake. David figured he and his dad would make the trip again later that year.

Harold stopped as he approached the Hall of Fame. It reminded Shelley of her pilgrimage to The Wall in Jerusalem years earlier. "I had read about it all my life," she said. "It is the basis of my faith. When I saw The Wall from a distance, I was overcome to actually believe I was going to walk up to it and touch it. It was a significant benchmark in my life."

In Cooperstown Harold stopped on the steps.

Maybe he was overwhelmed by the joy of having arrived. Maybe he was wishing that David could have been there with him. Maybe he was thinking of his own father, who had died when Harold was eighteen, and how when Harold missed him as a young man he would go to the ballpark and watch games, as the two of them once had.

Harold stopped and sobbed. His wife hugged him. Allan shook his hand. They were all crying by that point.

"I never thought I'd make it," he said.

"He lost his father at an early age, too," said David. "Sometimes he used baseball as a crutch when his dad wasn't around. Baseball fulfilled so many of his needs and going to Cooperstown completed that part of his life."

There's much that could be told of Harold's hours among the artifacts, of him lingering by Kaline's plaque, of him getting his picture taken near Ty Cobb's, of exhausting himself while exploring every inch of the museum in a manual wheelchair. But his story is like that of most pilgrimages. It isn't so much about what you do when you get there. It's not even about what you see. It's about everything that has brought you to that place. It's about the journey.

Since his father's death, David has been on a journey of his own. After two years at a lucrative job in corporate finance, he concluded that life was too short for seventy-hour work weeks. He began doing contract consulting and more vigorously pursued his passion for umpiring baseball games. Someday when the feelings aren't so fresh he will go to Cooperstown, maybe with a future son or a daughter. And he will stop at the steps before entering the Hall of Fame and someone watching may wonder why.

Let them wonder.

We take pilgrimages to connect with something sacred, something that—or someone who—touches our lives deeply. We go to be nearer our gods, whether spiritual or cultural or familial, whether at Mecca or in Jerusalem or at Mount Fuji—or at Graceland or Cooperstown.

By contrast, when we go to an ice-cream parlor, we just want ice cream.

And, in my brother's case, a bib.

14. Tyrus, Dear Boy

Mike Veeck brought his family to Cooperstown in 1999 with business partner Bill Murray, the comedian. Veeck wanted his seven-year-old daughter, Rebecca, to see the Hall of Fame plaque of her grandfather, legendary team owner Bill Veeck. Cooperstown was one of several stops—the Grand Canyon, Disney World, and Mexico being others—on a father's mission to fill his daughter's memory with "as many visual postcards . . . as possible"—before retinitis pigmentosa stole her sight. They had a great visit, according to Tim Wiles of the Hall Library.

Dad wakes Friday morning before either of us, and lays in bed for a half hour, just thinking, his eyes open and staring at the ceiling as if it were a movie screen. He wants to let us sleep longer. That's what he says later anyway.

When I was a boy and he'd be driving me somewhere in the gold Nova and I'd be looking out the window at nothing, he'd say, "A penny for your thoughts." Even then, thirty years back, those words sounded dated, like the music that accompanied the silent adventures of the Keystone Kops. As dated as when Dad jokingly yelled "dibs" as I gobbled a Milky Way candy bar with no desire to share. Or as when Mom would nuzzle beside me and whisper-sing, "Oh my darling, oh my darling, oh my darling, Clementine . . . ," as her stepfather used to sing to her.

"A penny for your thoughts," he would say.

And it's never easy to catch a thought even if you want to share it. They flit and flicker, they disappear as quickly as they arrive. You can think a dozen of them in a moment, scattered and disconnected, impossible to retrace let alone explain. Or maybe you're thinking how much you hate Blythe Topelsky, the sidearm show-off who struck you out twice and beat you to Cooperstown, and you're dreaming some future scene where you perform brilliantly and you embarrass him to tears and everything from there on out goes your way and he shuffles off into a miserable life. But you don't want to tell your dad that, you don't want him to know you think such ugly things. Or maybe you're looking out the window and you're envisioning Diane Sutametti in second hour and you're imagining what she looks like swimming naked and you've got your science book laying across your lap like a rectangular fig leaf and you're feeling every line in the road as the Nova bumps along the pavement and he says . . .

"A penny for your thoughts. . . . What are you thinking about?"

"Nothing!"

What I didn't realize then, but do now as a father of three boys ages twelve to sixteen, is that he wasn't asking for my thoughts. He was asking to be more of my life, to be closer, to be included, to not be shut out. He was asking for intimacy, though it's a word he would never use.

When all three of us finally awaken, Dad heads into the bathroom to shave.

"Be careful," Joey says. "The floor's slanted and slippery."

"Okay," Dad says. He closes the door.

I slept on a folding cot last night, and they shared a king-size bed.

"I never realized how small Dad's getting," my brother says. "He seemed tiny next to me."

It's the first night we have spent together in a hotel room since the 1960s, back when Dad was powerful and sturdy. I used to ask him to make a muscle and then try to link my hands around his bulging bicep, over the crater scar where he had received a smallpox vaccination. I would squeeze his muscle. It felt as impenetrable as rock. But he's shrinking now, as do men his age. He's getting smaller, and he makes light of it. "Back when I was five-ten . . . ," he says.

Joey heads downstairs and across the street to Stagecoach Coffee, and I find myself wondering what pictures played on the ceiling screen as Dad lay in bed this morning, just thinking.

Scenes of his Depression-era childhood, with his older brothers Clem, Bucky, and Teddy, two of them now passed? Times with his Pa, pruning the apricot tree, listening to Ty Tyson broadcast the game, sipping home brew? Of those sandlot hits off Hal Newhouser? Of the first look at Mom?

When I picture his memories, I see black-and-white photos, Brownie-camera still shots. But he sees them in color and the people move and talk and have personalities and opinions, some that grate, some that please. They come to life.

Was he revisiting our childhoods? Thinking of when Joey and I were boys, of playing running bases out in front of the birch tree on Shawn Drive? Was he thinking maybe he did all right? Maybe we turned out okay? Was he proud? Even at forty, you want your dad to be proud.

If I asked him, he would tell me. These later years have given him an openness that wasn't always there. Last night after the ice cream, he waited for his moment, for a pause in the conversation, for a spot that felt right. "I want you both to know that I'm really enjoying this," he said. "This is very special for me."

The year is 1902.

"Tyrus, Dear Boy," begins the letter, from a father to his son. "The first snow of the year of account is down today. It is two inches I reckon. It is all of a round fine hail not a single feathery flake."

The letter appears on the stationery of the Board of Education of Franklin County, Georgia, where its author, W. H. Cobb, served as school superintendent. It is dated January 5, 1902, roughly two weeks after Tyrus's sixteenth birthday, and it does not mention baseball, though one needn't look far beneath the surface to realize that Professor Cobb would prefer his son pursue another vocation.

"To be educated," he writes, "is not only to be master of the printed page but [to] be able to catch the messages of star, rock, flower, bird, painting and symphony. . . . Be good and dutiful, conquer your anger and wild passions that would degrade your dignity and belittle your manhood. Cherish all the good that springs up in you. Be under the perpetual guidance of the better angel of your nature. Starve out and drive out the demon that lurks in all human blood and [is] ready and anxious and restless to arise and reign. Be good."

Within three years, the senior Cobb was dead, allegedly shot by his wife who had reportedly mistaken him for a burglar. His son reached the major leagues weeks later.

There is another letter—several letters, in fact—in Ty Cobb's file at the Hall of Fame Library, this one from the retired ball player, dated 1935, to a third party. It relates to Cobb's oldest son, his namesake.

"I see by a postcard that Ty Jr. has been there with you all for a few days so I wanted to know if he made any kind of a loan or wanted to." Cobb writes that his oldest son failed prep school and college and six times ran up debts. "Ty has been a disappointment to me."

Dale Petroskey lives across from the National Baseball Hall of Fame. His son's room, he tells visitors, is the only boy's bedroom in America with a window that looks out at the entrance of the Hall of Fame. It's a view that he knows a million men like him would have loved as children.

At age five in 1961 Petroskey first heard the names Kaline, Mantle, and Maris. That summer he met Tiger Stadium. "From that moment forward, I knew that baseball was something I wanted as a big part of my life." How big, he could not have guessed.

It started as it often does with sandlot games and church leagues and heroes in hometown uniforms and it grew through junior high school with a volunteer job at the ballpark and a spot on two Kowalski Sausage national championship teams. It continued into college where he made the JV squad and into a summer league where Petroskey played with ten young men who would rise to the big leagues.

"I was facing a ninety-five-mile hour fastball from Bob Welch and I was not seeing it," he says. "I knew I wouldn't be hitting major-league pitching."

But his passion for the game endured. With a friend and a younger brother, he started the Mayo Smith Society in 1983 while working in Washington, D.C. They drew twenty transplanted Michiganians to the first breakfast meeting. The gathering blossomed into a fan association that at its peak had three thousand members, all Tiger supporters.

Before coming to Cooperstown, Petroskey lived near the nation's capital. He had worked in politics since the early 1980s, serving as assistant press secretary under President Reagan and as a senior spokesperson for a cabinet member. In 1999 he left an executive position with the National Geographic Society to lead the Hall of Fame, a job he described as too glorious to even dream of landing. That summer he and wife Ann moved from the fast-paced D.C. suburbs to quaint Cooperstown with their children Kathleen, Frank, and Claire, then twelve years and under.

"Our family had a chance to make a huge change away from traffic and the bigness of everything," he says. "There is no four thousand-student high school here. But there are three museums, an opera house, good schools, and a wonderful hospital, and we can walk everywhere. Not only was the job great, it was a chance to simplify our life as our kids were entering their teenage years. It boiled down to what's most important. This is a small town blessed with so many advantages because of the philanthropy of the Clark family through the years. It's a town that cares very much about preserving what it has, a town that realizes that almost every other place in America is changing and doesn't want to get swept along."

Sometimes while working in his yard, Petroskey will look across the street at the people arriving at the Hall of Fame. "It's young fathers and young sons; it's older fathers and older sons; and more and more mothers and daughters. You can see their excitement. They have a real sense that they're touching the spiritual and intellectual center of the game right here."

A framed pennant of Mayo Smith's 1968 Tigers hangs in Petroskey's office, along with a picture of President Reagan aboard Air Force One wearing a Detroit Tigers cap. There's also a shot of a national championship team, on which Petroskey played with future professionals Todd Cruz and Lary Sorensen.

Bill Haase, another Hall executive, joins us in Petroskey's office.

One topic leads to another, and soon I'm telling about Dad's sandlot hits off a teenage Harold Newhouser in a 1938 scrimmage. "They were bloopers," Dad admits. "But they all look good in the score book."

"I know what you mean, Joe," says Haase. "Those bloopers have a way of straightening out over the years."

The day will be hectic for Petroskey and Haase, greeting and entertaining Hall of Famers, rehearsing events, trying to ensure that everything goes perfectly. Our visit must be an intrusion but they treat us as if we are the most important event on their schedules.

Petroskey talks about the Negro Leagues and how it took

thirteen seasons before every major-league team integrated and how the Yankees passed on Willie Mays, one official remarking, "He doesn't look like a Yankee to us."

He talks about the Abner Doubleday myth. "As we like to say here, if the game wasn't invented in Cooperstown it should have been." And he recalls a dinner party he was invited to in Charlottesville, Virginia, to meet a best-selling author.

John Grisham grew up in Arkansas listening to Harry Caray broadcast St. Louis games. Anyone who has read his book *A Painted House* knows that Grisham admires Stan Musial. Petroskey brought the Cardinal legend to the party. "Grisham just about fainted," says Petroskey. They stayed five hours. Musial, who plays harmonica, brought one for the author. It was a night to remember.

Grisham, who named a son for Ty Cobb, owns a baseball complex with six fields. He serves as league commissioner, grooms the diamonds, and makes the schedules. Before the party, Musial visited Grisham's park and played an impromptu game of pepper with a *National Geographic* photographer that Petroskey had invited along. Then Musial—who had appeared on twenty-four All-Star teams and won seven batting titles and three World Series rings—said something Petroskey will never forget. "You know, Dale, watching my grandkids play now is more joy for me than playing baseball myself."

The words resonated.

"It's a game around which relationships are built," Petroskey says. "And they are generally the dearest relationships we have. To our parents, our brothers, our sisters, to friends."

15. Green Fields and White Porches

> **"V**isitors to Cooperstown who don't know a blessed thing about the game stop at Doubleday Field just to look at the ground, as deeply hallowed to baseball as Kitty Hawk, North Carolina, is to aviation."
>
> —Ken Smith in
> *Baseball's Hall of Fame*

Wedged along Main Street, the tiny Cooperstown Diner has a hand-painted sign on its roof and a yellow *Daily Star* news box out front. It is a cozy neighborhood place with door chimes that ring when customers enter. Its half-paneled walls hold a hodgepodge of framed black-and-white group photos from the 1950s or 1960s, maybe of suited Hall of Famers or Rotarians or members of the ivy-covered Mohican Club next door. A Pepsi board on the wall lists sandwich options: fish on a bun, $2.95; tuna melt, $3.40; Steak-umm, $2.95.

The dining area can't be more than ten by twenty feet, and it is nearly full when we arrive. We take the only open table and order breakfast. Some locals—distinguished from the tourists by their lack of cameras and baseball regalia and by the fact that the waitress knows their names—are grumping about politics.

"They told the town fathers to hell with you and moved it just across the county line," says one.

"They're a bunch of yum-yums," another says.

George Jones is playing on the radio.

"I'm glad I came," Joey says.

Though we planned the trip months in advance, it looked as if it might fall apart at the last minute when my brother changed jobs. He had been with his new employer only a few weeks, and it seemed frivolous to be taking unpaid vacation so soon with college tuition about to come due for two of his children. He told his wife about his reluctance.

"You big dumb idiot," she said. "What, are you stupid? How many other chances do you think you're going to get? Go on the trip."

The food arrives, and Dad pours ketchup between his hash browns and scrambled eggs.

"What a nice man," he says of Dale Petroskey.

"That was amazing," Joey adds. "You imagine the busiest time at your job and then to take that much time to be that friendly. That was something."

They're impressed with Petroskey, and I read their comments to mean that they think I have special pull, which I don't. "He's involved in an annual Mayo Smith Society gathering at Comerica Ballpark each summer," I say. "You get to play catch on the field and tour the locker room and meet players. We should go."

Dad splashes more ketchup on his hash browns.

"A group from my church goes to the park each year," Joey says. "There's a big event called Home Plate, with people from churches from all over. There's a prayer service before the game and some speakers. We could go to that sometime. You know, if you want."

The conversation has edged close to religion, a topic that, like politics, we usually avoid out of respect for our differences, I like to think.

In such matters Dad has changed little in my lifetime. He has been consistent in his beliefs. It's been awhile since he attended church for anything other than holidays, funerals, or weddings, but he sees himself as a Catholic, a Polish Catholic. Those early years spent as an altar boy at Holy Name Church forever shaped his self-image.

Politically he's always been a Democrat, though he doesn't pressure us.

"Do what's best for your family," he told me before the Bush-Gore election. "If you need to vote Republican for money reasons, that's what you should do."

But I seldom vote Republican, and Joey often does, which surprises everyone who knew him in 1972. About the time I started admiring his liberalism, he was drifting from it, focusing more on raising his young family than correcting injustice. Gone were the speeches about Vietnam and Indian rights and the death penalty and the legalization of marijuana.

A few years back I realized how different we had become politically. The subject was income tax.

"It's legal robbery," he said. "I figured it out. Four of every ten hours I work are just to pay the government. That's twenty weeks of the year."

"Well, nobody likes taxes."

"Between state and federal, they take about forty percent. That's ridiculous."

"Well, we do get something in return."

"But it's our pay, not theirs. We're the ones working for it."

Money has never struck me as a romantic cause, not when compared to ending war, racism, and inequality—the issues at the heart of my brother's early activism. I have this glorified picture of him as an eighteen-year-old fighting the righteous battle, and it remains at the very core of how I see him today, even if he has strayed. I like to get him talking about his high school days, his opposition to the draft, as if talking might reignite a dormant liberalism. Those days, however, trouble him.

My brother's political conversion was gradual. Yet there's no doubt where he stands today—opposite me on many issues.

About religion: Dad used to take us to St. Malachy Church. The neighborhood around Shawn Drive was young then, and the church had no building of its own. The parish met in the cafeteria at Frost Elementary School. We went for a while but stopped around the time Mom got sick. Joey had made first communion and gotten to eat the wafers. I never did. Church disappeared abruptly from our lives.

Two decades later I joined the congregation in which my wife had been raised. We made friends there but eventually quit going. Afterward, my brother became involved in a church that encourages members to spread the word. "You get to a point where you look at your life and you see you have a wonderful family, a good job, decent pay, a nice house, nice things, and you still feel like you're missing something," he has said.

He's much more fervent in his beliefs than I am. So I try

not to talk about that stuff with him. And about the most he says, unless asked, is that his church will be taking a trip to the ballpark and we could go to that sometime. "You know, if you want."

I'm torn. Though I'd like to share the event with my brother—though I'd like to support him in a facet of his life that has brought him great joy—I don't want him to misinterpret my attendance. I don't want to become his personal conversion project.

And, too, there's a thought that whispers deep inside me, a fear really, that traces itself to my childhood when I hungered so much for his attention, a fear that it could still be within me to change my life, my faith, to please my brother, who has no idea how much and in what ways he has influenced me.

I have trouble saying no to him. Fortunately, he doesn't ask much of me.

Cooperstown feels like other well-preserved, modestly well-to-do villages. A few blocks off Main Street away from the lake, narrow sidewalks bump over tree roots and stretch through shady neighborhoods where tourists rarely travel. Children in helmets ride bikes, gray-haired men prune trees, and a woman in a bathrobe stands in her drive watching, a cup of coffee in her palms.

There are white porches all along Elm and Eagle and Walnut and Beaver streets and all throughout town. If Dr. Seuss had visited Cooperstown, he might have been inspired to write, "There are small porches and big porches, some open, some enclosed. There are porches with flags, lamps, benches, and roses. There are porches on hills and porches that wrap around homes. There are porches with spindles and columns and stones. I like porches, I like them indeed, I like them with wreaths done in dried flowers and tweed."

Farther from Main Street, behind the elementary and secondary schools, are two ordinary ball fields where children play league games. The town also has a men's over-thirty fast-pitch hardball team. On some weekdays early in summer when the sun nears the hills and casts long shadows across the diamond, you can hear them trying to recapture the magic of days gone by as wives, girlfriends, and children watch from the metal bleachers, as a fly ball floats into left field and finds the ground and a teammate yells from the bench, "Come on, Johnny. Put some oil in your knee brace. You should have had that." And Johnny answers, "Ten years ago maybe."

In the grass a nondescript marker the size of a small gravestone notes that the field is dedicated to Stephen C. Clark. It is one of the only memorials to the family that has served as village benefactor for several generations. The most notable tribute is the Clark Sports Center, a modern facility that includes basketball, squash, and racquetball courts, swimming and diving pools, bowling alleys, running tracks, climbing walls, soccer and ball fields, a fitness center, and a ropes course. The Clarks underwrite the facility. The Hall of Fame induction is held on its grounds. Clark interests also fund Bassett Healthcare, the county's largest employer; control the village's three museums; award hundreds of scholarships annually to local students; own about one-fifth of all land in the area; employ 2,500 people; and contribute nearly $100 million a year in payroll to the local economy. Clark charities, most headed by Hall of Fame Chairman Jane Forbes Clark, donate more than $6 million a year for a wide variety of projects—from flowers to fire trucks.

Every small town should be so lucky.

Across from the Cooperstown Diner and down aways stands a bronze statue of the Sandlot Kid, a farm boy in wide-brimmed hat and overalls, with a bat clenched in his hands. Doubleday Field is just beyond. The sculpture honors the notion that baseball came to be in the former Phinney pasture now occupied by Doubleday Field—or, if not there, then in one of a hundred other small villages.

Doubleday Field preceded the Hall of Fame, not only in myth as the place where Abner Doubleday transformed a game into something uniquely American but in actuality by roughly twenty years. Back when Ty Cobb was winning batting titles— before anyone had considered locating a baseball museum in Cooperstown—the village acquired land for the ballpark. It was partly out of need, partly out of a desire to pay tribute to the national pastime, and maybe even out of embarrassment. In 1915 the village baseball diamond at the fairgrounds had been demolished for new construction. Consequently, the town that laid claim to being baseball's Garden of Eden had no formal field.

The chamber of commerce led the effort to build Doubleday, hoping to draw tourists through the town's new train station, where portraits of the general and James Fenimore Cooper greeted travelers. The first official game at the new Doubleday Field didn't take place until August 1919. Four years later, village taxpayers voted to buy the land from the chamber. They erected a wooden grandstand the following year.

The Phinney lot had been chosen because Abner Graves—the same man who promoted Doubleday as the father of baseball—had mentioned the site as one of many where the game took place. But, Graves once admitted, "I do not know, neither is it possible for anyone to know, on what spot the first game was played according to Doubleday's plan."

Still, efforts to raise funds proclaimed the lot as the sport's cradle. A plea for donations that appeared in *Baseball Magazine* around 1920 hyped the effort in this manner: "Tucked away in a little town in New York state lies a vacant field which should be dear to the heart of every baseball fan. For it was the site of the first diamond on record. The architect of that rude square, the forerunner of every ball field on earth, was Abner Doubleday. And this waste lot was the scene of the first consistent effort to standardize the sport which has captivated all of English-speaking North America and has its ramifications throughout the inhabitable globe. Think of it! There was a time less than a hundred years ago, when only one rough unkept diamond looked up to the sky with its message of cheer and health and wholesome exercise. . . ."

The park, independent of the Hall of Fame down the street, has changed over time, getting a brick grandstand in the 1930s through a works project and sets of bleachers in 1960 from Red Sox owner Tom Yawkey. It has become historical in its own right, hosting stars like Ruth, DiMaggio, Musial, and Charlie

Gehringer. It even appears in the movie *A League of Their Own,* and it is a stopping point for visitors. This morning the parking lot holds cars from Virginia, Ohio, Texas, New Hampshire, New Jersey, Pennsylvania, California, Georgia, Florida, and Massachusetts, the last with a SAVE FENWAY PARK! sticker on its bumper.

In the covered stands behind home plate, a few girls bounce up and down gray-painted steps imprinted with cleat marks that resemble bird scratches in the sand. The wood grain shows through in sections.

"Sarah, this used to be a real, real, real old field," a girl in shorts tells her younger sister. "The sign when we came in said THE BIRTHPLACE OF BASEBALL. It's where the first game was played, right Dad?"

"You betcha," he says, panning his video camera over the field, from the brick dugouts to the quaint scoreboard in left to the bleachers in right. The landscape beyond the outfield bursts with trees, homes, and church steeples, the park snug against the neighborhood.

A young man with orange hair takes in the view with his father, a bearded academic type in khakis and wingtips. "There's not a bad seat in the house," the son says.

Up higher, two boys in uniforms survey the parking lot. A man with an Hispanic accent calls to them, "Okay, guys. We got to get back to the bus."

In three days a game will take place here between the Milwaukee Brewers and Florida Marlins. The professionals come once a year. But kids take swings on this diamond throughout the summer.

"Did you ever play on a field this nice?"

Dad considers the question. Near the pitcher's mound, a crow caws.

"Mack Park had wooden stands and a wooden fence around it," he says. "It was a rickety place but it felt like a big deal."

Turkey Stearnes played at Mack Park, home to the Negro League Detroit Stars of the 1920s. A center fielder, Stearnes hit mammoth home runs. His talent got him elected to the Hall of Fame last year. He died poor; a number marks his grave, twenty miles from my home.

"Now Bucky, he played at Tiger Stadium when it was Navin Field. He was an outfielder. A heck of a ball player. Ran like a bull, powerful but fast. Man could he get down that base path."

Dad looks out at Doubleday Field as if he can see his brother, a young man again, charging to first. Bucky will turn eighty-seven in September. He lives near Los Angeles and walks with a cane.

Uncle Bucky in the Land of Legends—I have heard the story before. In high school Bucky played in a championship game at the major-league park. He got to cover the same outfield as Cobb and Heinie Manush and linger on the dugout steps and twirl two bats above his head in the on-deck circle and saunter up to the left side of home plate and barrel down the base line when he hit the ball.

The dirt diamonds of my youth were unremarkable, no-frills suburban fields with bases, backstops, and splintered benches. Until the summer of my twelfth year, I thought all kids played on fields like that.

I learned the truth in July 1973 when we drove to Kansas

to visit Mom's family. It was another world. Some relatives lived on dairy farms, some in stone houses, none in subdivisions like ours. They raised pigs and cattle and grew corn and raspberries. They talked with accents, and the boys wore their hair short, contrasting my in-style, shoulder-length shag cut.

"You look like a city slicker," said my cousin Dean.

His friend had a less favorable impression.

"He looks like a girl," he said.

I met Dean at a ball field after his team had finished a late game. Dusk hung on the horizon, and lightning bugs flashed in the distance against a dark backdrop of trees. But the ball field shone beneath lights—lights!—the whole thing rimmed in fence, with an infield of grass, a raised pitching mound, a warning track, and a scoreboard just beyond.

My cousins' lives seemed old-fashioned and backward. But their ball field was greener than my envy. It was the pride of a small town, and the vision of it comes back to me here at Doubleday Field, where the close outfield fences make for cozy confines: 296 feet down the left-field line, 312 to right.

At the annual Hall of Fame game, players regularly belt balls out of this park. Double-digit scores are common. Some blasts even plunk the roofs of houses beyond the park.

"I'm glad I never had to pitch here," Don Sutton said the year he was inducted. "Boy, I would've given up a ton of home runs."

16. Summer 1972:
The Home Run

We often played our St. Malachy games at Wilde Elementary, named for a school official, not the writer. There wasn't much to the ball field. It had a cyclone-fence backstop, a brittle diamond that got grated and chalked weekly, and a patchy green outfield that ended 400 to 800 feet from home plate—at a parking lot in right, at Bunert Road in center, and in left at the six-foot fence that enclosed the backyards of the houses that bordered the playground. But by game time, with our fathers home from the tank plant or General Motors or Chrysler and watching from foul territory with our mothers on their blankets and in their woven lawn chairs, it felt as if we were the center of the universe.

ABOVE: Charlie Gehringer *(Detroit Public Library, Burton Historical Collection)*

The sun shone brightly on our games. Isn't that how we remember the sterling moments of our youthful summer times, as taking place in the sun? How could it be otherwise?

It says something about my playing abilities that my best game occurred when I was eleven. But like Denny McLain, I peaked early. On that late afternoon I had caught two fly balls in center, singled and scored on Frankie Perzanowski's double, and tripled in Jeff Mancini for another run. But the true glory awaited.

With two runners on I hammered a sidearm pitch from Blythe Topelsky. I say hammered but when you truly connect, when the wood barrel of your thirty-inch bat meets the ball perfectly, you don't feel it. You swing through it, and it soars. And it did, over the left fielder's head, well beyond him, and I ran wildly, rounding first wide, making sure to hit second, and feeling flush as my teammates screamed and as my dad, behind the backstop, clenched the fence and twitched his legs as if running the bases with me and as Coach Rychlewski windmilled his arms at third base and yelled, "Come on, Stanton!" The ball rolled a long way and only made it back to the infield after I had crossed the plate and been swallowed in a crowd of cheering teammates. I could hear my manager's voice over the noise. "Save some of him for me!" he yelled. I could see my dad clapping, and it felt glorious. I felt like Johnny Bench, who had hit seven home runs in five games. I felt like Willie Horton and Al Kaline. I felt destined for Cooperstown. I felt as wonderful as I imagined my brother always felt, with his good grades and his own car and his art awards and his pack of friends.

We St. Malachy Tigers celebrated our victory at 7-Eleven,

sucking down Slurpees from white plastic tumblers imprinted with portraits of Bill Stoneman, Jim Lonborg, Maury Wills, Willie Stargell, and Joe Pepitone.

That night in bed as the sounds of *Marcus Welby, M.D.* drifted from the living room where my parents watched television, with Mom savoring a glass of beer into which she sometimes cracked a raw egg and with Dad snacking on a cheese-and-ketchup sandwich and with their distant voices occasionally interrupting the soft life-and-death words of Robert Young and James Brolin, I lay beneath fresh white sheets, the dirt from the ball field showered from my ankles, the success of the day—the thrill of it, its promise—still washing over me.

Cool air seeped into the darkened room from the cracked window. Ernie Harwell and Ray Lane were broadcasting the late game from Oakland. Joe Coleman was pitching for us, "Catfish" Hunter for them. I could see the A's in their green-and-yellow uniforms, their faces brandishing mustaches. I could picture each of our hitters and most of theirs—Rudi, Reggie, Bando—as they came to the plate.

Ernie filled the innings with anecdotes, recalling "King Kong" Keller or Rogers Hornsby or Joe Bauman, who hit 72 home runs in one minor league season. He sent birthday greetings to folks back in Detroit, reading their names and ages; he expressed his wishes that some longtime Tiger fan have a speedy recovery in the hospital; and he worked in a plug for Marathon Oil, one of the sponsors.

Some nights I had trouble falling asleep. I'd lie on my back, eyes open, staring toward the ceiling, staring so hard into the darkness that I could see tiny red and blue dots buzzing nervously above me.

"Think pleasant thoughts," Mom would say.

So I'd think about baseball and the Tigers winning and Willie Horton hitting home runs. I'd dream about becoming a bat-boy, befriending Al Kaline's sons, getting rides on Mickey Lolich's motorcycle, laughing at Norm Cash's jokes, and hanging out at the ballpark, with its green seats and green dugouts and green field. I'd imagine myself playing in the major leagues and hardly ever making an out and breaking Joe DiMaggio's record and Babe Ruth's and Ty Cobb's, too, and winning the World Series and appearing in All-Star Games with Johnny Bench and, unlike that greedy Vida Blue, not caring how much money they paid me and being gracious about my immense talent, like Charlie Gehringer who always took the first pitch and loved his mother. I'd think pleasant thoughts about Cooperstown, how nice it would be when we finally went, Dad and me and maybe Joey if he changed his ways, and how far it was from Warren and how different it would be from our town, how perfect it would be to escape there.

It never occurred to me that we might not make it that year. My father, after all, had said "maybe" while watching the home opener with me and he had bought me a book filled with photos of the game's greatest stars and now he had seen me hit my home run, seen my teammates swarm around me. He had seen me as a hero. There was no question: My father would be taking me to the Hall of Fame.

"Think pleasant thoughts," Mom would say.

In Cooperstown, I imagined, everyone was happy. Why wouldn't they be? Their days were filled with sunlight and ice-cream cones and wooden bats and baseball, and that would be enough to supply you with pleasant thoughts all throughout the day and to push away—bury deeper—those worries that tried to surface at night no matter how many pleasant thoughts you crammed into your mind, worries that you would never confess to your friends, about your brother maybe going to Vietnam now that he had graduated from high school, about your mother returning to the hospital. Because Jim O'Connor's brother was missing. And Ty Cobb's son had died of a brain tumor. And Josh Gibson had one. And Walter Johnson, too.

You don't know that it's going to be all right at the time. You don't know that until it's past and over and your mom's home from the hospital. You just know that she keeps having these surgeries and that your aunts and uncles tell everybody how unfair it is—"Betty's had more than her share"—and that the school counselor puts her arm around your shoulders more than anyone else's and that your friends' mothers keep saying how sad it is and that they tell you how they're sure she'll be fine and you agree but don't really know because you remember when Johnny Woitha went in the hospital and never came back. And you try to think pleasant thoughts because they're so much better than the other ones. Because when you think about death and you allow the possibility that nothing comes after it—that everything ends when you die, that you never live again, ever—it frightens you to your core.

After Al Kaline put us ahead 2-1 in the fifth, I surrendered to the weight of my eyelids and I thought pleasant thoughts. It was easy that night, with the home run and all.

Sometime later after the house had quieted, Dad came into my room, closed the window, and reclaimed his transistor radio. When filled with worry and unable to sleep, he often lay in the spare twin bed. It would be easier on Mom, he reasoned. She needed her rest and, besides, that way he would be near when I awoke calling out in the night.

17. Williams, Feller, and Prince Hal

> **"T**here have been two memorable moments in
> this happy life of a baseball ambassador, two
> special days. One was when I was inducted
> into the Baseball Hall of Fame. The other was
> when I married Anne."
>
> —Bob Feller in
> *Now Pitching: Bob Feller*

Where do they hide the McDonald's?" Joey wonders.

There is no McDonald's. No Tim Hortons. No Motel 6. It's not that fast-food restaurants and hotel chains don't want to be here; they do. The town—as well as the Clarks, bless them—just discourages them. McDonald's and Pizza Hut have tried to come. But Clark representatives, wanting to preserve the village's charm, squelched their plans by purchasing land targeted for development. (Big Macs and Personal Pizzas are available miles down the road near Cooperstown Dreams Park, a complex that draws thousands of young players and their families for weeklong tournaments.)

Baseball businesses dominate Main Street. They're tucked in tasteful red-brick buildings, and their names leave no doubt as to the nature of the town: America's Game, National Pastime, Our National Game, Bottom of the Seventh, Seventh Inning

Stretch, Extra Innings, Third Base: Last Stop Before Home, The Home Plate, Cooperstown Bat Company, The Where It All Began Bat Co., Mickey's Place. There is a Doubleday Café and a Short Stop Restaurant. Of course, there's a bank or two, Sal's Pizzeria, and a few other places. But they're in the minority, scattered among stores with windows displaying score books from Ebbets Field and Comiskey Park, flannel uniforms, honey-colored bats and shellacked balls, Yankee pennants, Kirby Puckett posters, photos of Mattingly and Ichiro, and flyers advertising an endless string of autograph sessions by visiting Hall of Famers and Pete Rose. One sign notes that Willie Mays will be signing "flat items" for $120 apiece.

"They shouldn't be doing that this weekend," Joey says.

"What's that?"

"Charging for autographs," he says.

My brother collects signatures. He has thousands, most acquired through the mail for the price of postage stamps. He doesn't sell them, he saves them. He writes former players and asks about their careers, the greatest feats they witnessed, and whatever else strikes him.

"I'd love to be playing now with the high salaries," wrote Phil Rizzuto, "but we had more fun." He signed his note "Scooter."

Johnny Sain included a flyer with press clippings. Virgil "Fire" Trucks sent a business card imprinted with a red fire truck. Bobby Thomson—in an act of humility or oversight—said the greatest feat he witnessed was Mark McGwire's 62nd home run (not his own "Shot Heard Around the World"). Earl Weaver asked for a $20 charity donation. A former home-run champion signed a card and requested a $3 check in his name.

Killebrew, Kaline, Aaron, Banks, Berra, Jeter—they all signed. Senator Jim Bunning's office declined with a form letter noting that he had been inundated with requests. "His time must be spent representing his constituents." And one of "Catfish" Hunter's relatives wrote a year before he died, "Mr. Hunter cannot do autographs now. He is having problems with his hands. Thanks for being his fan."

In this one respect at least, my brother followed me. I was the one sending off those letters in 1972—gushier versions of them, letters that began, "Dear Willie, I am your biggest fan. You waved to me against the Royals. I was wondering . . ."

We pass a line of tables along Main Street where players wait for customers. There's Enos "Country" Slaughter and Monte Irvin looking more boyish than his eighty-some years and a very round Gaylord Perry, who with mustache resembles a Civil War colonel.

Nearby, an older gentleman rests on a shaded bench facing the parking lot of Doubleday Field. He sits beneath a basket of geraniums as red as the "B" on his Sox cap. "That looks like Bobby Doerr," Joey says. "He sent me an autograph."

Doerr wrote that his most memorable moment was watching The Great Ted Williams in the 1941 All-Star Game. Doerr had started at second for the American League, leading off ahead of Cecil Travis, DiMaggio, and Williams.

For weeks prior to the July 8 contest, DiMaggio dominated sports headlines with his hitting streak. On June 29, he surpassed George Sisler's league record of 41 straight games with a hit. On July 2, he broke Wee Willie Keeler's major-league mark of 44. And he kept on going, taking his streak to 56 games—57, if you count his All-Star double—before the run ended July 17 in front of 67,468 fans in Cleveland.

DiMaggio's feat overshadowed Ted Williams's fine season. But the Boston slugger, who would hit .406 that year and win the home run title, upstaged DiMaggio at the Midsummer Classic, the first one played in Detroit.

Pirates shortstop Arky Vaughan had put the National Leaguers ahead 5-3 with two-run home runs in the seventh and eighth innings, and the senior circuit appeared en route to its second consecutive All-Star victory.

Cubs hurler Claude Passeau opened the ninth inning by retiring catcher Frankie "Blimp" Hayes. Ken Keltner, batting for White Sox lefty Eddie Smith, drove the ball past the shortstop. Joe Gordon, Doerr's replacement at second, followed with a single and Passeau walked Travis to load the bases.

DiMaggio hit a hard grounder, a likely double play, to short but Travis's slide into second disrupted Billy Herman's relay to first. Keltner scored, Gordon went to third, and DiMaggio stood on first.

That brought Williams, the twenty-two-year-old cleanup hitter, to the plate. Williams had fanned against Passeau in the eighth, taking a called third strike. He vowed not to let it happen again. "Listen, you lug," he told himself. "He outguessed you last time, and you got caught. Let's swing a littler earlier this time and see if we can connect."

On a 2-1 pitch, Williams blasted a high fastball into the upper deck in right, giving his team a 7-5 win. "I've never been so happy," he said. "Halfway down to first, seeing that ball going out, I stopped running and started leaping and jumping and clapping my hands and I was so happy I laughed out loud."

Decades on, Williams cited that home run as his most memorable.

Bob Feller—who pitched three shutout innings in that game and charged onto the field in street clothes to celebrate Williams's heroics—barrels out of a store in front of us. Dad recognizes him.

Before joining the Navy, Bob Feller dominated the American League, leading in victories and strikeouts from 1939 to 1941. After Feller enlisted, Hal Newhouser, who was ineligible for military service because of a heart murmur, developed into an overpowering starter. He topped both leagues in victories and strikeouts in 1944 and 1945, winning back-to-back MVPs and leading the Tigers to a world title.

Feller returned to the majors in August 1945 and sought to reestablish himself and to end rumors that he had lost his fastball. Newhouser also had something to prove. Critics had marked his wartime performance with an asterisk, noting that Prince Hal had risen to prominence during the absence of Williams, DiMaggio, and fellow sluggers. He was no Feller, some said.

Their first postwar showdown came August 24 when 46,000 celebrated Feller's return. He did not disappoint. Feller four-hit the Tigers, struck out a dozen, and beat Newhouser 4-2. The next week, Newhouser prevailed and the Tigers went on to win the World Series. The rivalry might have ended there had New-houser drifted toward mediocrity in 1946. But he didn't.

That same year Dad and Mom opened a small, storefront restaurant, Stanky's Eat Shop, in Atchison, Kansas, birthplace of Amelia Earhart. The town, memorialized in the song "Atchison-Topeka-Santa Fe," overlooks the Missouri River.

My parents had no children and lived in a downtown apartment. Their diner served pork chops and fried chicken. Grandma Muse sat at a table by the front window to create the illusion that they had customers. They advertised their "clean sanitary kitchen" and "friendly, quick service" in the *Atchison Daily Globe* across the street. Their ad appeared next to Bob Hope's joke column.

The Browns and the Cardinals, the closest major-league teams to Atchison, played in St. Louis, 270 miles away. The Kansas City Blues, a minor-league squad, also had a local following, and there was affection as well for Bob Feller, a onetime farm boy from rural Iowa.

But Newhouser's fan base in Atchison consisted of one man, my dad, who followed Prince Hal's achievements in the papers.

By September 1946 the Indians and Tigers were out of the pennant race, well behind Bobby Doerr and the Red Sox. But their aces, Feller and Newhouser, were locked in a battle with Boston's Dave "Boo" Ferriss for the league wins title. (Each had twenty-five.) Looking to boost their gates, the Indians and Tigers agreed to pit Feller and Newhouser against each other on successive Sundays. They had not faced off since the previous season.

The first matchup came on September 22. Cleveland owner Bill Veeck advertised it as "The Pitching Duel of the Century," drawing 38,103 to Municipal Stadium. Before the game Feller and Newhouser posed for photos, shaking hands and smiling at one another. Detroit manager Steve O'Neill compared it to the historic battles between Addie Joss and Big Ed Walsh.

Newhouser pitched impeccably, shutting out the Indians 3-0 and expending just 98 pitches—72 of them strikes—over nine innings. Feller lacked control.

The rematch a week later took on added significance with Feller pursuing the season strikeout mark. More than 47,000 turned out on a rainy day in Detroit to watch him break Rube Waddell's record. Newhouser lost the game but finished 26-9, compared to 26-15 for Feller. He came within twenty-seven votes of an unprecedented third straight MVP. (Ted Williams got the honor, and Doerr finished third.)

Stanky's Eat Shop closed in 1947 before the freeway came through Atchison. Dad went to school under the GI Bill to study photography in Kansas City. In 1953 he and Mom moved back to Detroit and started a family. The Tigers, meanwhile, released Hal Newhouser, who had developed arm trouble. The former sandlot star returned for the 1954 season with another team. He was signed by General Manager Hank Greenberg, and went 7-2 with a 2.51 earned run average, appearing mostly in relief— as a Cleveland teammate of Bob Feller.

In Cooperstown nearly half a century later, Bob Feller darts across Main Street right in front of us. We pause and nudge each other. But before we can manage a word, he's gone—as quick as one of his fastballs.

What I notice are his oversized eyeglasses, the same kind my father wears.

"Feller and Newhouser used to have some big battles," Dad says.

18. Mickey's Numbers

"It *was the biggest honor of my life when 89.1 percent of the 415 members of the Baseball Writers Association voted for me."*

—Frank Robinson in *Extra Innings*

They call it the Hall of Fame Records Room, and it has black, back-lit walls that illuminate the names of pitchers who won at least two hundred games and hitters who belted three hundred or more home runs. (Willie Horton's on that list.)

It's a place that invites arguments. One fan may see that Dave Kingman hit 442 home runs and wonder aloud why he's not in the Hall of Fame like some below him: Duke Snider, Al Kaline, and Johnny Bench.

Another may remember that Kingman batted in the .230s, hardly a sign of excellence and a good sixty points shy of Kaline. And that explains that.

But what about Dale Murphy? He hit more home runs than Bench, got more hits, scored more runs, had a similar average, won a comparable number of league titles, and, like Bench, accumulated some Gold Gloves.

Impressive, but Murphy played outfield. You can't compare catchers to outfielders. A Hall of Fame outfielder needs to hit over .265 to distinguish himself.

Oh, like Reggie Jackson?

You're not seriously comparing Dale Murphy to Reggie Jackson—to Mr. October—are you? Jackson has five World Series rings. What's Murphy got? None! End of discussion.

All right, but what about Dwight Evans? Why isn't he in? Almost all of his numbers are better than Ralph Kiner's.

They should be. He played twice as many years. Kiner played ten seasons, yet he won seven National League home-run titles.

Yeah, but Kiner was the best player on bad teams. Only once did he finish above fourth place. Evans performed in the clutch. Doesn't that count for something? And how do you measure spirit and leadership? Did you see the catch he made in the eleventh inning of Game Six of the '75 Series? He turned Joe Morgan's home run into a double play.

Look, only Babe Ruth hit dingers more frequently than Ralph Kiner. So leave him out of it. If you're building a case for Dwight Evans, then what about Ron Santo? There's a guy who has a strong argument. Or if you want a Red Sox player, how about Jim Rice? He's more deserving than Evans. Or Steve Garvey. His team won a World Series, after all.

Few topics divide fans more than who belongs and who doesn't in the Hall of Fame.

There are no rigid criteria. The rules say a player should be retired for five years and have played ten seasons in the majors. But those requirements can be waived. Lou Gehrig was inducted in 1939, the year he left the game; Roberto Clemente in 1973, after he died. And Addie Joss played just nine seasons. (Tubercular meningitis took his life at age thirty-one in 1911.) Every eligible player who has collected three thousand hits, five hundred home runs, or three hundred wins has made it to Cooperstown. But it's not written or required. There is no guarantee. Nothing would prevent voters from snubbing one who achieves such marks.

Selection is subjective and imperfect.

The controversies started with the first election in 1936. Baseball writers were to choose players from two categories, those from the 1800s and those active from 1900 to 1935. (There was no rule barring current stars.) Of the latter-day legends, Ty Cobb, Babe Ruth, Honus Wagner, Christy Mathewson, and Walter Johnson were chosen. But those voting for the old-timers did not give any candidates the required three-fourths approval. Absent from the list of inductees was Cy Young, the game's only 500-game winner, who having played in two centuries drew votes in both categories but lacked enough support in either. Young was picked the following year.

The voting procedure has changed repeatedly. Now prospective Hall of Famers receive recognition in one of two ways: from the Baseball Writers' Association, which elects players who were active up to twenty years ago, and the Veterans Committee, which considers everyone else.

No matter how it's done, the outcome stirs debate.

Earl Averill spent most of his career with Cleveland in the 1930s. His disappointment over his long wait for induction surfaced in his acceptance speech.

"I thank those who supported my election," he said. "However, I'm convinced my record speaks for itself and that I was qualified to become a member. . . . My disagreement with how the Hall of Fame elections are held and who is elected is not based on bitterness, that I had to wait thirty-four years after retirement to receive this honor. It is based on the fact that statistics alone are not enough to gain a player such recognition. What right does anyone have to ignore cold hard facts in favor of looking for some intangible item to keep a person out of Cooperstown?"

Averill hit .318 over his career when the league batting average hovered around .280. Reaching that level in the 1930s wasn't nearly as impressive as doing it in the 1960s when league averages fell into the .240s. In 1934 when Averill hit .313, the Tigers team as a whole hit .300. When Carl Yastrzemski led the league in 1968 at .301, Oakland players topped the Americans with a .240 team average. Yastrzemski, thus, had a much better season than Averill, even though Averill's average was higher.

Baseball statistics have evolved to the point where we can more accurately gauge players' contributions and more fairly compare those who played in different eras and benefited from specific ballparks. There are ways to level the playing field statistically and to earnestly measure player performance.

Consequently, some fans argue that opinion be bleached from the selection process, that induction be based on specific credentials. The new statistics are useful tools. But I recoil at the thought of replacing human judgment with sterile methodology. We'd just find ourselves debating mathematical formulas rather than the talents of the players we witnessed. Like Jack Morris.

Morris should be in the Hall of Fame," my brother says. We're studying the lengthy roster of the 200 Victory Club, and find Morris's name listed with Red Faber's at 254 wins and ahead of Carl Hubbell's at 253 and Bob Gibson's at 251. Faber, Hubbell, and Gibson have been inducted into the Hall.

"You know, Morris won more games in the '80s than any other pitcher," Joey says. "He won the World Series with three different teams. He should have a plaque here."

"Too bad he wasn't a nicer guy. That might have helped."

"Very competitive," Dad adds. "But maybe that's what it takes. Newhouser was the same way."

Hal Newhouser is on the list with 207 victories. He retired in 1955 and debuted on the Hall of Fame ballot in 1962. For thirty years he waited to be honored as one of baseball's best. "Not a day goes by that I don't think about it," he said. "It bothers me."

In 1988 he sent letters to members of the Veterans Committee. "I just wanted to find out if there was a reason for me not making it." No one wrote back.

Each year on the day when the committee would announce its decision, he would sit by the radio and hope for good news. It came finally in 1992. He was seventy-one. He called his ninety-five-year-old mother, and they both cried. She saw him inducted that summer.

Newhouser, incidentally, stayed in baseball as a scout through the mid-1990s. He urged the Astros to make Derek Jeter their first pick and when they took someone else, he quit. He had tamed his intensity but never lost it.

"I don't see Tommy Bridges," Dad says, squinting at the list. Bridges's name isn't here.

The man whom Red Smith once described as "about as big as thirty cents worth of liver" accumulated 194 victories. Bridges tried desperately to reach 200, giving up his coaching job in 1946 for one last spring on the mound. Perhaps he hoped that two hundred wins would bring a measure of immortality. He would have had no illusions about it qualifying him for the Hall of Fame. At the time only four pitchers had been inducted: Walter Johnson, Cy Young, Christy Mathewson, and Grover Cleveland Alexander—and all had at least 373 wins.

"I want to win two hundred games," said Bridges. "I figure I'm a cinch to do it."

But he wasn't. Bridges lasted nine games before he retired again, relinquishing to Bobo Newsom his status as the day's winningest active pitcher.

"My pa really liked Tommy Bridges," says Dad. "Bridges was a little guy like him and he threw sharp curves. Pa got a kick out of how Bridges could fool the big hitters. Oh, he thought Bridges was great."

Somewhere on the list between Jack Morris and Hal Newhouser is another Tiger.

Dad notices.

"Mickey Lolich," he says. "Two hundred and seventeen wins."

When you're a kid and you've played just three seasons yourself, you don't grasp the notion of excellence over time. You've not yet lived through Mark Fidrych, and so you have little appreciation for how quickly it can fall apart. It's tough to separate the Nate Colberts from the Reggie Jacksons. You see Colbert hit five home runs in a doubleheader and 38 over a season and you imagine what will happen if he keeps doing it for fifteen years. At that pace he might break Babe Ruth's record. Or what about Earl Williams? In 1971 and 1972 he looks as good as Johnny Bench and you read in *Sport* magazine where Hank Aaron predicts he might be better than Bench. "I expect him to hit maybe thirty-five or forty home runs for seven or eight years," Aaron says, and you think Williams is on his way. But he's not and neither is Colbert and soon their numbers fizzle and they're out of baseball.

Which wasn't the case with Mickey Lolich. Like Bridges, he pitched sixteen seasons and was a force in most of them. But he truly sparkled in only a few, and I remember him for those. Isn't that how it works, that we picture our heroes at their best, that our childhood devotion blinds us to their weaknesses? For me Lolich will always be the guy who won three games in the 1968 World Series, dominated the league in 1971, led us into the playoffs in 1972, and served as ace of our pitching staff throughout my childhood.

When the Tigers traded him for Rusty Staub, I was fourteen. The following spring I wrote the New York Mets, telling them how fortunate they were, how Mickey would serve them well.

If you wrote such letters before everyone started enclosing baseball cards to be signed, you know that teams often responded with cheap photos and preprinted autographs. Evidently Lolich's batch had yet to arrive, for someone took a Polaroid of him and he signed it with a blue ballpoint pen. Lolich looked peculiar in a striped uniform, smiling beneath that foreign NY cap, his pitching shoulder branded with a patch of the Manhattan skyline. His sideburns were grayer.

I have the photo yet.

Lolich became eligible for the Hall of Fame in 1985, the year my son Zack was born. But he got his most votes in 1988, when my twin boys, William and Taylor, arrived. Lolich attracted 109 votes that year—212 shy of induction—and his support dropped dramatically afterward. Now his hopes rest with the Veterans Committee, and I suspect that's where they will die.

Earlier this summer the post office issued a series of stamps honoring America's classic ballparks. Because my previous book was about Tiger Stadium, I was invited to speak at the unveiling of one of the stamps. Mickey Lolich was there as well, and organizers sat me next to him near home plate on the ball field.

He didn't recognize me from our doughnut shop encounter eighteen years earlier. I didn't think he would.

"Do you speak after me?" Lolich asked.

"I hope not," I said. "That would be anticlimactic. You should hit cleanup."

His arms were crossed atop his ample belly, and he nodded in agreement, confirming how right I was.

I wish I had ten victories to sprinkle throughout Lolich's career. I would give him two more in 1964, three in 1968, one in 1969, and four in 1973. Then he would have six 20-win seasons—not two—and maybe others would see him as I remember him, as a Hall of Famer.

19. August 1972: The Showdown

The seventh-floor waiting room at Beaumont Hospital looked out over a parking lot that on a Tuesday in early August was wet with rain. Everything about it whispered. There was no television, just cushioned chairs and couches and homey lamps that gave the curtained room a soft, sleepy glow. The reading material consisted of tattered issues of *Highlights for Children* and an abundant supply of hardcover books featuring illustrated Bible stories.

Dad brought Colleen and me to visit Mom two days after surgery. We stopped first in the fragrant, flower-filled gift shop, where he treated us to a box of Andes mints, thin slabs of chocolate heaven wrapped in Christmas-green foil. "Share,

---

ABOVE: Brothers Tom and Joe Stanton *(Joseph Stanton)*

and don't eat them all at once," he said as he headed to her room.

By Mom's sixth craniotomy Colleen and I knew the routine. If Mom felt well enough, she would return with him to the waiting room, shuffling down the hall in her slippers and robe, Dad on one side bracing her, the wheeled IV stand on the other, clenched in her left hand, the scepter of the frail. If not, he would return alone and try to sneak us into her room. No one under fourteen was permitted. But occasionally a nurse would say nothing or pretend not to see our familiar faces. Or Dad would plead ignorance.

That evening the nurse at the counter never looked up as I walked taller on my toes and tried to keep my tennis shoes from squeaking on the flecked tile floor. It was a solemn walk to Mom's room. The mournful moans of an elderly man filled the hall, blending with the electronic chatter and canned laughter of several televisions. Colleen toted her Barbie doll and held tight to Dad's hand. I clutched the mustard-yellow transistor radio on which I had hoped to hear the rain-delayed Tigers-Brewers game.

I looked into darkened hospital rooms as we passed, and my eyes met those of a hollow grandmother who was out of bed and silhouetted ghostlike by light from the window behind her. I turned away and stared at the floor and then felt ashamed, realizing too late that she had smiled.

No matter how many times you see your mom with her head shaven, the sight shocks you. It might have been different if she had been bald all the time, but between surgeries her black hair would grow back—first prickly short, then like a brush cut, then stylish in a Sandy Duncan kind of way, then long enough so she could set a few curlers, and then it would be time for another operation and she would be as bald again as she was that night, with the surgeon's freshly stitched, horseshoe-shaped incision hidden beneath a gauze wrap that favored the left side of her skull.

Her eyes perked when she saw us.

"Happy birthday, Mom."

We eased ourselves between the safety bars on opposite sides of her elevated bed. She pecked us softly on the lips, and we took care not to bump her head.

It was her fiftieth birthday, and we had made a card of blue construction paper and silver glitter. Dad had brought two cans of Altes beer, pulled the tab on one, and gave it to her. It was part of the ritual. He brought beer after surgeries. "Hell, she deserves one," Dr. Latimer had told him.

"How are my hotsy-totsies?" Mom asked, her voice thin.

"Hotsy-totsies"—the word came from a song she had been singing since we were little. It was babyish but we were in the hospital and didn't complain.

Mom asked Colleen what she had done that day, about adventures with friends, about stray animals or injured birds she might have come upon.

She asked about my St. Malachy team, forgetting that the season was over.

"Oh, that's right. Well, how are your Tigers doing?"

"They beat Boston. It was on television. It was the Monday night Game of the Week. They're in first place and Mickey Lolich got his eighteenth win."

"Wow!" she said, trying to sound excited.

"If he keeps that up," I added, "he could be going to the Hall of Fame."

Dad's shoulders tightened. He sensed where this might be heading. He knew how easily my good intentions could be derailed. Mom's surgeries brought out the worst in me. Dad probably remembered that during an earlier hospitalization I had slugged Roman Rizzo in the stomach at school while Ron Perkanski held his arms behind his back.

Dad narrowed his eyes at me, trying to will my silence.

I hadn't planned on pressing the Hall of Fame issue at the hospital. But such things had a way of surfacing. Summer was disappearing and with it any hope of going soon. School would start in a month, and then we'd have to wait a year. That's a long time when you're a kid and you can remember most of your Christmases and count almost all your birthdays on your fingers. With Mom being sick again and Joey having gotten a low draft number, everybody had forgotten about Cooperstown. Everybody except me.

"Maybe when you're all better and you get out, we can go to the Hall of Fame," I said, my voice perky, as if the Hall of Fame were something she would enjoy, her reward for enduring another surgery.

Dad preempted Mom, his voice hospital-quiet but stern, that mixture parents use when they want you to know they mean business but don't want other adults to know how nasty they can get.

"I've already told you, we can't go this year."

"No you didn't."

"Yes I did."

"Un-uh."

"Well I'm telling you now. We're not going."

Mom danced her good fingers through my hair.

"We never do nothing I want."

"Tommy," Dad said through his teeth, as if beginning a thought. But he said nothing more.

"I'm sorry it's been so rough on you two," Mom said.

J oey drove us home that evening. Dad stayed at the hospital, sitting in a chair and reading the *Detroit News* beside Mom as she slept.

Rain pelted the canvas roof of my brother's red Austin-Healey Sprite, nearly drowning the sound of Three Dog Night singing about Jeremiah the bullfrog. Joey had one hand permanently on the steering wheel and the other going from the wheel to the Kool cigarette pressed between his lips to the tray brimming with butts, where he dropped ashes with the flick of his middle finger. He had bought the car from a guy at the butcher's shop where he worked, and had marked its bumper with a MCGOVERN sticker, which was replaced with a MCGOVERN-EAGLETON sticker, which after Eagleton withdrew was replaced with a MCGOVERN-SHRIVER version, which outlived the car itself.

The little vehicle jerked when he shifted gears and shook when he drove fast. Approaching stoplights, you felt as if you might slip under the truck ahead of you. But you also felt cool, driving with your brother in a car that made other people look.

The ball game resumed after a long rain delay. The Brewers were far ahead, and both managers, Billy Martin and Del Crandall, were aware at the start of the fifth inning that a rainout was possible. Crandall tried to get the inning over by having his players swing at bad pitches and overrun bases. Martin's men tried delay tactics—pickoff throws to first when the runner hadn't taken a lead, an unnecessary pitching change, refusing to catch an easy-out pop-up. Martin didn't want to accept the defeat, and I could relate.

I thought of asking Joey to take me to Cooperstown. But I knew he had more pressing matters in his life. He had become a man and I remained a boy, and it felt as if it would always be that way, that our lives were destined to be unequal, he always ahead of me, I always on the other side of the backstop. In a couple weeks Joey would start art classes at the community college and then a job as a custodian at a children's hospital. He and his girlfriend had begun planning their wedding. His life was accelerating as mine stalled. He had gone from being one of us kids playing at Frost School to someone more like a parent, driving and smoking and being in charge of me.

It was dark, and the wipers struggled to clear the windshield. We could barely see through the downpour but one thing had become clear. I wouldn't be going to Cooperstown anytime soon.

20. What Matters

> **"I**t is a ghostly feeling, standing chest-deep in history here at the Baseball Hall of Fame. We tour the museum until our ankles swell. Salinger has never been here before. I have."
>
> —Ray on stopping in Cooperstown with writer
> J. D. Salinger in W. P. Kinsella's novel *Shoeless Joe*

My brother lingers over Ty Cobb's diary. "It really gives you some insights into his life," he says.

On its lined pages in his handwriting, Cobb recorded almost daily entries for January 1946. The journal, though brief at less than six hundred words, provides a glimpse of Cobb at age fifty-nine. His competitive spirit, his preoccupation with money, even a blunt recognition that he drinks too much—they're all here, along with a roster of famous names.

He talks of winning $3.50 off Walter Hagen in a game of golf. He remarks that he needs to see G. Hearst about keeping his divorce settlement "out of headlines." He records encounters with Grantland "Granny" Rice, Mickey Cochrane, Harry Heilmann, Joe DiMaggio ("he can't putt for big money"), and

Tris Speaker—"asked Spoke how a .345 hitter got into the Hall of Fame"—and he remembers that he owes Ernest Hemingway a letter.

He starts the year taking phone calls, "not collect," from soldiers overseas. He laments losing a lucky golf ball on the thirteenth hole and two bats from his locked garage—"cops no help." Cobb notes when he buys a couple of cases of Old Forrester whiskey and, the next day, dinner for a friend. "My treat," he says. He celebrates the success of his Coca-Cola and General Motors stock and his payoff at the horse races, wagering $200 on King Tiger in the eighth. He also describes Cincinnati as a "horseshit town."

"Drinking too much," he writes on January 10.

"Stayed sober," he says sixteen days later.

There's evidence of his generosity: a $2,000 gift to Cochrane for surgery, $200 to an orphanage, $800 to an old-timers association, all recorded in his handwriting.

But it's the three mentions of Babe Ruth that draw my attention. He recalls showing promoter Christy Walsh his 1926 $85,000 contract with Connie Mack, "which beat Ruth," he adds. He basks in the glory of United Press International naming him top player of the half-century. "Best thing was," he boasts, "I beat out Ruth."

Between those two entries is one more somber.

"Heard from Cochrane," he pens. "Ruth seriously ill . . . may be strikeout for him."

The diary gets my brother thinking.

"It's kind of sad," he says. "Does he even mention his children?"

There is one entry about son Herschel. "Doing good in Twin Falls. Grossed $135,000 over past two years."

Ty Cobb and his wife Charlie, who first filed for divorce in 1930 and finally went through with it in 1947, had five children: Ty Jr., Shirley, Herschel, Beverly, and Jimmy. It's widely recognized that Cobb was toughest on his namesake, who preferred tennis to baseball, playing the gentlemanly sport at Princeton before he flunked out, and later captaining the Yale team, where an undergraduate degree eluded him. Ty Jr. did become a successful physician but he died young in 1952 at age forty-two. (His brother Herschel had died a year earlier.)

Ty Sr. and Ty Jr. never connected as adults, though the father made an effort near the end, visiting his dying son at his ex-wife's home in California. By that point a cancerous brain tumor had eroded the son's short-term memory. He sometimes did not recall what he had said a moment earlier.

"Mr. Cobb came to see him," his daughter Shirley told the *Augusta Chronicle*. "Ty Jr. and Mr. Cobb were talking about dogs and hunting. I heard my father say, 'I'll give you one of those.' Ty momentarily forgot my father was even there. He turned away and said, 'Shirl, he will never give me anything.' [My father] was stunned. He went over to the window and looked out. Then he walked out of the room, and he never came back again. He couldn't have done that any more than he could have said he was sorry."

Late in life Cobb expressed regrets. "When you get older," he said, "you wish for companionship."

Cobb's diary touches my brother. "I wouldn't enjoy that life," he says. "You think it's glamorous. But I would never want that kind of life."

He's talking about the life of a ball player, not the life of Cobb.

"Really?"

"Well, they're on the road so much, gone for chunks of the year. They have to miss a lot," he says. "When you're looking at people like that, you have to wonder what happens with their family life. Do they sacrifice their families for success? I'm not willing to make that sacrifice. Look at the plaques in the gallery. Those guys are there because they played baseball better than anyone else. That's all. It doesn't say how they treated people or that they were good to their wives or children. It doesn't say how many birthdays and anniversaries they missed."

"They're not saints," I reply. "But many of them are decent. Kaline, Gehringer, Lou Gehrig."

"Yeah, I know. I'm just saying they had to pay a price and sometimes it was steep, sometimes it was the other people in their lives."

On one level we're talking about ball players. But it strikes me that if he changed a few words, he might be talking about me. Does he realize it? When I was building a newspaper business I spent way too many hours at the office working months straight without a day off, often topping eighty hours a week.

Dad has been silent during the conversation, and—we thought—oblivious to it. "I worked too many Saturdays when you were growing up," he says. "I shouldn't have worked so many Saturdays. I should have spent more time with you kids."

His words catch us by surprise. Our father devoted himself to taking care of our mother and us, and he never complained. He has nothing to regret.

"You spent a lot of time with us," Joey says.

"Yeah, you've always been there," I add.

Dad shrugs his shoulders, embarrassed that he's provoked praise.

"Well, at the time," he says, "it's not so simple to tell what matters most."

Two twenty-year-olds from Brooklyn are faithfully reading the exhibits.

"I'm learning too much," one says.

"Yeah, I know," says the other, in a Mark Leiter jersey. "It's starting to hurt my head."

Wandering through the museum, you can't help but overhear the words of others—and sometimes be drawn into them.

"Hang on, Dad," says a boy, grabbing his father's elbow. "I didn't see in here."

"Yes, you did. That's Babe Ruth's stuff."

"I don't remember seeing any of this."

"You saw it all, Tiger."

They walk back into Ruth's room anyway.

In the Hank Aaron exhibit, half of it devoted to other players who have hit more than five hundred home runs, a young coach with bleached hair points to a picture of Harmon Killebrew unleashing his swing. The coach has an entourage of nine-year-olds. "Hey guys, where's his front foot pointing? Where's his belly button pointing?"

"The pitcher," the kids answer in rough unison.

Nearby a father and daughter stand before Ty Cobb's dental work.

"You never heard of Ty Cobb?" he asks. "He's one of the greatest."

"Are those his teeth?"

"Part of them."

And then there's a guy playfully trying to impress his wife. "I can tell you everything about baseball," he boasts.

"Who invented it?" she asks.

"Oh, ah, what was his name, umm?"

He looks at me.

I give the short answer, figuring he doesn't want the whole story. "Abner Doubleday?" I say, making it sound like a question, to plant some doubt.

"Yeah, that's it. Doubleday," he says.

"Oh, Doubleday Field," she adds. "Okay."

Down a ways, a man in a Polo shirt stands alone before a Cardinal-red locker containing a cap, jersey, and stool. He stares at the items for the longest time. "Stan Musial," he says softly, to himself.

It would be possible to be cynical at the museum. You could look at the remnants of Crosley and Forbes fields and get yourself muttering about the anonymous places that replaced them. You could drool over the cigarette cards from the early 1900s, with their stark orange, red, and sunset-gold backgrounds, and lament how investors hijacked the hobby. You could shake your head at the primitive fingerless gloves worn by the game's pioneers and head off on a rant about today's ball players being pampered.

But wouldn't it be better to be standing amid the display of sheet music, with the lazy summer sounds of Terry Cashman's "Talking Baseball"—". . . Kluszewski, Campanella . . . The Man and Bobby Feller. . . ."—wafting through the chilled, dimly lit corridor as you look at the tattered cover of the curious love song "Remember Me to My Old Gal" that features a photo of Philadelphia's Chief Bender, Jack Coombs, and Cy Morgan? It was written by George Moriarty, a Tiger in the time of Cobb, and it reminds you of your grandfather, who came to America in that era, starred in the holiday stories of your father and aunts and uncles, and died three years before you were born.

You don't have to embrace the place with blind, unfettered romanticism. There are, after all, reminders—the Black Sox Scandal, the segregated Negro Leagues, Pete Rose—that the sport is as imperfect as the people who have occupied it throughout history. But why would anyone visiting Cooperstown decide to be sour about the price of souvenirs, an occasional wait in a line, or the search for a parking space? It's better to let all that slide around you, like Cobb around a tag.

Joe E. Brown."

Dad's voice is flush with surprise as if he has run into a forgotten friend. We are in the Baseball at the Movies exhibit, and he has his eyes on a shadowy photo of a comedian with an eggplant-sized mouth.

"Looks like Joey," I say.

My brother doesn't respond.

The still shot is from the movie *Alibi Ike,* one of three base-ball films that featured Joe E. Brown from 1932 to 1935, Dad's early teen years. In the photo Brown is pitching for the Rose-dale Rosies and his throwing arm is above his head as if he's about to windmill the ball to the plate.

"Did you see that movie?"

"Oh, I must have," he says. "We used to walk to the Fron-tenac Theater or the Eastown all the time. In those days it cost a nickel or dime to get in. . . ."

It would be a Saturday or a Sunday, and Dad would be eleven or twelve and he would be tagging along with Teddy, the closest in age of his five brothers. Teddy would be walking with a buddy, and Dad would be keeping a respectful distance be-hind them, like a courtier following a king.

"He hated to take me but that was his job."

Sometimes Teddy would snitch an apple from a grocery stand as he sauntered past.

The Frontenac was a mile or two from their home, and their route took them by St. Cyril Church and the neighborhood of Uncle Steve and Uncle Bruno. "You're the spitting image of your Uncle Bruno," relatives told Dad. Uncle Bruno had a large goiter on his neck.

"I'd look in the mirror at my big left ear sticking out from my head and then imagine that I had a goiter, too," Dad says. "I'd think, 'Gosh, I hope I don't look like Uncle Bruno.' "

The Frontenac Theater wasn't as fancy as the Eastown, which had a balcony, stuffed chairs, and uniformed ushers. The Frontenac sometimes smelt of urine because boys would pee on the sloped floor rather than walk to the restroom. But the candy bars were as good—monstrous Mounds bars that in Dad's tales were as big as bricks.

"They'd show two movies and cartoons and a newsreel and previews and maybe a serial with Tom Mix or Buster Crabbe."

Dad couldn't remember whether he had seen *Alibi Ike* or *Elmer the Great* or *Fireman, Save My Child*. In all of the films Brown stars as the pitching hero, winning the big game. In two of the movies, he rebuffs gamblers who would have him throw the championship.

"He used to make a kind of yelp when he pitched," Dad says.

Brown's face looks familiar to me, probably etched upon my memory in childhood when I'd wake early on Sunday mornings and watch the dated black-and-white comedies that ran on a local station. Some were silent films, with the Keystone Kops, Charlie Chaplin, Buster Keaton, or Harold Lloyd. Others featured Laurel and Hardy or the Marx Brothers.

Dad would be up already, making coffee for him and Mom, and he'd join me in the living room, adjust the antenna for a better picture, settle on the couch beside me, and we'd both get to laughing—a duet of chuckles, his in bass, mine in soprano—as Lou Costello tried to figure out who was on first. Among dozens of Sunday-morning movies we watched, we must have shared one starring Joe E. Brown.

We didn't go to theaters often but he did take me in 1973 to see *Bang the Drum Slowly*, a story about a baseball friendship. Robert De Niro plays Bruce, a dense farm-boy catcher on the verge of being cut by the Yankees. Only his best friend and the star pitcher, Arthur, portrayed by Michael Moriarty, knows he has leukemia. Arthur negotiates his contract to ensure that

Bruce gets to spend his final season in the major leagues. In one scene the two friends are fishing along a stream near Bruce's boyhood home in Georgia. The rim of Bruce's ball cap is flipped up and he's got a chaw of tobacco in his cheek. "Arthur," he says, "tell me why in hell I swam up and down this mud a million times and I never drowned and why I never got killed from the war in Vietnam or why I never got plastered by a truck but I come clean through all that and now I get this disease."

Photos from *Bang the Drum Slowly* hang in the museum.

"You took me to see that movie," I say.

Dad squints at the shots of De Niro behind the plate and on the bench and in the locker room.

"The Roseville Theatre?"

"Right."

Everywhere in the museum it is like that.

In the exhibit honoring legendary announcers, their taped voices calling games decades ended, we think not just of Red Barber and Mel Allen and Ernie Harwell and their verbal music but of Uncle George anchored in his favorite chair on a summer evening with his angry little bristle-furred dog Pepper on his lap, tense and loaded with growl, and with radios on each side and four games going at once, plays crackling over the air from Cleveland and Pittsburgh and Chicago and, of course, Detroit, and Uncle George knowing the score of all of them.

Or we see Grantland Rice's manual typewriter, and it evokes another era, the New York of the 1920s and 1930s, of Rice and Ring Lardner and Damon Runyon and Heywood Broun. It reminds us of Uncle Clem, who loved so much the idea of being a writer and of drinking with writers, who talked of books and art and who left Detroit during the FDR years for New York's Greenwich Village to return not long after, his fiction folio filled with rejections from *Esquire, Coronet,* and *Stag* that said the same thing: "Sorry, not our style." The same Uncle Clem who, forty years later when we were boys writing baseball newsletters that we copied on cheap paper and distributed at family gatherings, would contribute columns of his own, treating the enterprise with all the seriousness we imagined it deserved.

Or we see Sam Crawford's shoes and we think of our Grandpa Stankiewicz; or we spot a mention of Bill Veeck and remember how he answered our letter after the Bicentennial saying that he would be happy to field a female player; or we admire Kaline's jersey and remember some long ago visit to Tiger Stadium with our father and our brother.

Or we note in the display on Don Larsen's perfect game that the last out was made by Brooklyn pinch-hitter Dale Mitchell, the same Dale Mitchell that Coach Ed Rychlewski had bragged about way back when. "That guy could hit," he had said.

I grew up about a mile from Walt Whitman Branch Library in Warren, and Dad often took Colleen and me there in the evening. It was air-conditioned. While my sister looked at books about animals and Dad browsed car-repair manuals, I gravitated toward the 790s section. Then as now, you could find baseball books in the 790s in rows organized by Dewey decimal numbers. One heavy tome, *The Baseball Encyclopedia,* dominated the sports shelves. On its two thousand thin, delicate pages appeared the career records of every man to play in the major leagues.

That's where I found Dale Mitchell.

Like Mickey Mantle and Johnny Bench, Mitchell had been

born in Oklahoma. He played eleven years in the majors, all with the Cleveland Indians, save for the final months with Brooklyn. His last at bat came against Don Larsen. Three times his average placed him among the five best in the American League. In 1948 only The Great Ted Williams, Stan Musial, and Lou Boudreau had higher averages. Mitchell played on three World Series teams, sharing rosters with Feller, Lemon, Early Wynn, Satchel Paige, Doby, Campanella, Pee Wee Reese, Duke Snider, and Jackie Robinson. He batted .312 over his career—higher than Kaline. Coach Ed was right: "That guy could hit."

The Baseball Encyclopedia was a reservoir of information, and it could entertain you for hours. You could turn the pages back to 1931 when, like you, your dad was eleven. You could see who led the American League in hitting (Al Simmons) and home runs (Ruth and Gehrig) and wins (Lefty Grove got 31) and you could see that the Tigers were lousy that year, finishing second from last, and that Marty McManus, whom Dad never talked of, played third base. You could look among the list of lifetime batting leaders and discover Ty Cobb's name atop more categories than Ruth's. You could check out Hal Newhouser. You could check for Jimmy Reggio, one of your dad's teenage friends who reportedly made it to the minors. You could flip through the player register and count all the guys named Stewart who had unusual nicknames—Ace, Bud, Neb, Stuffy, Tuffy, Bunky, Lefty, and Mack. You might even get distracted when you came upon Tom Sexton and just for the heck of it check out other intriguing names. Cannonball Titcomb. Bill Dickey. Bill Butland. Hank Boney. Charlie Fuchs. Tom Asmussen. And worse.

Sometimes the *Encyclopedia* raised as many questions as it

answered. Why did Bubba Floyd, who played in just three games and batted .444, leave baseball? What about Gail Henley, who went nine for thirty? Or Tom Hughes, hitting .373 lifetime in fifty-nine at bats? Wasn't that enough to keep him in the majors? Or John Paciorek, who might have been the best player ever based on his statistics? He never made an out. He played in one game, went three for three, got two walks, scored four runs, and knocked in three for the Houston Colts in 1963. And that was it, a perfect performance. What happened?

During the Depression, Dale Alexander led the league in hitting at .367 for the Red Sox but fizzled the next season and stopped playing after five years—with a .331 career average. Why? The statistics in *The Baseball Encyclopedia* did not explain. What about Willard Hershberger and Austin McHenry? Their careers ended suddenly in death. What tragedies befell them?

In time as you got deeper into the sport, those mysteries would be resolved. You'd read somewhere that Paciorek had suffered a career-ending injury. You'd hear an uncle talk about how Alexander's skills had diminished quickly, and you'd discover that Hershberger had taken his own life. And Austin McHenry, well, he had died of a brain tumor.

The curators of this museum may aim to tell the history of baseball, but the magic of the place is that we pick the pieces that illuminate our own stories, rekindle our warm tales, and illustrate our personal narratives.

21. Ben Caffyn and the Cleveland Naps

On *an August day in 1956, writer John McCallum drove Ty Cobb from New York City to Cooperstown in a car that Cobb had borrowed from Chrysler. An hour from the village, Cobb insisted that McCallum head twenty-five miles out of the way for a gas fill-up. The writer told the retired star that there were closer stations. "I know that," Cobb said, "but they give Green Stamps at the station down this road. I save them."*

From the second-floor walkway above the library and bookstore, Tim Wiles surveys the growing crowd below in the bright atrium beyond the statue of Mighty Casey at bat. This weekend will be the museum's busiest of the year, with 25,000 people in town to witness the induction of four men. For some visitors, it's an annual trip; for others, the culmination of a lifelong dream. All, from stars like Dave Winfield to ordinary fans like us, have a story to tell about how they arrived at this hamlet among the hills.

Few have taken Tim Wiles's path. His official journey began in May 1988. Wiles had graduated from the University of Iowa, earning a bachelor's degree in English with hopes of pursuing a literary career but with no immediate prospects and an uncertain sense of where the coming months would find him. He was on a friend's couch thumbing through *Sports Illustrated.* SUSPENDED! read the cover headline, stamped over a photo of Pete Rose. Inside, Wiles found a whimsical profile of Tom Heitz, an attorney who had gone from being a Vietnam-era judge with the Marines in 1972 to librarian at the Hall of Fame eleven years later.

"I called Tom and told him I wanted to work here. I was the thirtieth person to call that day."

"There's not an opening," Heitz said. But if there were, he advised, Wiles would need a master's degree in library science.

The next day Wiles enrolled in the Iowa library program. Seven years on, after completing graduate work, interning at the museum, and laboring in the university stacks, he joined the Hall of Fame staff, fusing two passions. "I have always loved libraries, and I have always loved baseball," he says.

Wiles grew up in Peoria, Illinois, as did his father, grandfather, and great-grandfather, Ben Caffyn. According to family legend, Caffyn had played in the majors. The record book confirmed it, recording his contribution on one line: 1906, Cleveland, 103 at bats, 20 hits, .194 average. He belonged to the Cleveland Naps, who were managed by and nicknamed for Nap Lajoie. Wiles knew little more than that as a boy.

"I never heard a specific game story. All we ever heard is that he had played for Cleveland. It was so little to go on that it whetted my appetite for more. I continually looked him up in the *Encyclopedia* and would see those statistics unchanged and figure that's all we would ever know. His story hung over our family in a very romantic way."

In 1898 at age eighteen, Caffyn had married a girl two years younger, and they had a son. But when her family discovered that the new father would be disappearing for a chunk of the year to play ball—a career deemed no better than riverboat gambler or carnival barker—her family got the marriage annulled and sent the child to be raised by relatives.

Caffyn died in 1942. His grandson, Wiles's father, was five and has no memories of him. The ball player left no gloves or balls, no baseball heirlooms, just family, descendants who loved the game but, in Tim's case at least, didn't play it particularly well.

"He seemed to be of such an ancient generation," says Wiles. "But it was always very valuable to me to know that he had made the majors." Wiles bragged to schoolmates about his great-grandfather, who competed against Ty Cobb. "If pushed, I could get out *The Baseball Encyclopedia* and prove it. But when your great-grandfather hits .194, the specifics are not something you necessarily want to bring up all the time."

I n the research library behind a closed door away from foot traffic, you find no shelves of books to peruse. There are tables, chairs, a counter, a copy machine, a microfilm reader, and a display on the late commissioner A. Bartlett Giamatti, a Yale president for whom the center was rededicated. Beneath the library are three infield-sized, climate-controlled, secured-access rooms. One holds photos; another, audio and visual recordings; and the third, print items. Nearly all materials are available to visitors. Some aren't. (Joe DiMaggio, for example, stipulated that the library could not duplicate photos of him with Marilyn Monroe.)

At the counter you request materials from librarians who

head upstairs or downstairs in search of them. They return by elevator or stairwell, carting red-covered issues of *Baseball Magazine* from the 1920s, Charlie Gehringer scrapbooks, obscure texts, or some of the over fifty thousand file folders that fill banks of cabinets. There is at least one folder for every man who played in the majors, and you must wear white cotton gloves when handling any of them.

Many days the library gets a hundred or more letters, phone calls, and e-mails from fans seeking information. Visitors wander through the door, curious for a peek. Historians and researchers make arrangements in advance.

Frequently someone will call or write wondering about an uncle or a father or a grandfather who played minor-league ball. The library has a quarter million contract cards, which track the careers of such men. The cards are often the only proof remaining to confirm a family story that has grown vague in the mist of decades. Those who made the majors get permanent entries in a baseball encyclopedia. No matter how small their contribution, they will be remembered. But recognition can escape minor leaguers.

Like Jimmy Reggio.

In the late 1930s my dad played Class D Federation ball in Detroit. He was a second baseman with the Rams, stationed across the bag from Reggio, who was a year younger and lived a street over.

"Jimmy was a likeable kid," Dad says, "a little taller than me, with dark curly hair. He hit from the left side, pretty unusual for a shortstop. But he threw right-handed."

The Rams' best players—Reggio, Dad, and Lou Burmeister,

a catcher who shot bullets from the crouch—hoped to be picked as extras for Roose-Vanker, a tournament-bound American Legion team. The squad starred Harold Newhouser, the hard-throwing sensation who had already been tagged as a big-league prospect.

"Who was our best player?" Dad asked, paraphrasing my question. "I thought I was."

But Roose-Vanker selected Reggio for the tournament, and Dad figured that his own abilities didn't match his perception of them. He realized then that he might never be a Detroit Tiger. Reggio ended up staying with the American Legion team and attracted interest from scouts. The last anybody from the old neighborhood had heard he was headed to the minor leagues with plans to make everyone forget Luke Appling and Joe Cronin.

At family gatherings during my boyhood, Dad and his brothers would inevitably get talking about their adolescent exploits on the playing field. "Whatever happened to Jimmy Reggio?" someone would ask.

"I don't think he ever-ah made the big time," Uncle Teddy would say, and they would all agree. I checked the record books as a kid, as Wiles had done for his great-grandfather. But there were no Reggios listed. No Regios or Riegos either. Nothing close.

My dad is full of stories like that, tales that begin half a century ago with somebody he knew—an uncle, a classmate—getting a tryout or an invitation, somebody with a hope of making it. I clung to them as if they were promises. But all of those tales, except for the one about Newhouser, end right where they start. His versions anyway. The names disappear into the obscurity of the minor leagues around the time of World War II and never reemerge into the sunlight of the majors.

Tim Wiles found Reggio's record among the contract cards. "James Reggio, 7112 Milton Ave., Detroit, Mich." someone had typed long ago at the top of the first card. There are three cards, front and back, with 73 entries that give dates and teams and status, with X's marked in columns noting whether he was under contract or released or assigned outright or reserved or disabled. Nothing says how Reggio played, just that he did and with a good many teams: Daytona Beach, Hamilton, Monett, Albany (Georgia), Lansing, New Bern, Ashland, Zanesville, Logan, Portsmouth, Nashville, Los Angeles, Albany (New York), Savannah, Macon, Columbia, Charleston, Burlington, and Sunbury. Like us, he also stopped in Toronto and Buffalo before he (rather, his contract card) made it to Cooperstown.

Dad's former teammate played in the minors from 1939 to 1952. He would have been in his early thirties before he surrendered the dream. His frustration must have grown as his prospects receded because Reggio got suspended three times in his final years—after ten seasons of staying on the good side of managers and officials.

In *Shoeless Joe*, the baseball classic that inspired the movie *Field of Dreams*, Ray Kinsella abducts writer J. D. Salinger and takes him on a road trip that ventures off the main highway to the museum in Cooperstown, where, says Kinsella, "there are so many strange and wonderful bits of information—things no one but baseball fanatics would care about. . . ."

Kinsella and Salinger find themselves drawn to the library. It's 1979, and they want to know about "Moonlight" Graham, whose career consisted of a half inning and no at bats. Clifford Kachline, the historian, pulls the file. It is thin, containing only one sheet, a questionnaire on which an elderly Graham says he would do it all over again if given the chance.

Salinger and Graham and Kachline are real people. Ray Kinsella, the Iowa farm owner, is not, though he shares the last name of his creator, author W. P. Kinsella.

In childhood, when I wrote the Hall of Fame asking about one thing or another—Ty Cobb, Mickey Lolich, baseball superstitions—a response always came from Clifford Kachline. A month ago at the annual gathering of the Society for American Baseball Research in Milwaukee, I met him, extending my right hand to shake his, remembering too late that his had been mangled in a long-ago printing accident. Kachline recalled the day author Kinsella came in search of "Moonlight" Graham. Indeed, Kachline had retrieved the player's file. But it was empty. There was nothing in it. The questionnaire came later, filled out by a family member, not by Graham as in the novel.

Tim Wiles may be the only person who has worked in the two libraries—one at the Hall of Fame, one at the University of Iowa—featured in *Shoeless Joe*. "I like to think of Kinsella taking a life that in a baseball context had been reduced to a single half inning defensively and bringing alive the story of the man's larger life to such a vast audience," he says.

Before he came to Cooperstown, Wiles inquired whether the Hall of Fame had any information about his great-grandfather, Ben Caffyn. There was no file material but Wiles collected what he could over the years, pursuing tips and searching the Spalding statistical guides that came out annually from 1877 to 1941. He learned that Caffyn had batted .353 in 1906 in the Western League. He discovered that the Welshman had brawled with his own manager at home plate after the manager accused him of performing poorly because of late nights carousing. "Caffyn will be disposed of by the Toronto club," reported *Sporting Life*. "When he is right he is considered to be a good man for the outfield."

Wiles added the clippings to his great-grandfather's file and it grew.

W. P. Kinsella's book and the movie that followed sparked interest in "Moonlight" Graham, who actually did become a physician, true to the fiction. Graham's file today features dozens of entries. It has grown to a half inch in thickness—about the same size as Ben Caffyn's.

Caffyn played in thirty games with Cleveland. That seems like not much of a start. But another outfielder, making his Naps debut four summers after, saw action in only twenty contests, and he—"Shoeless" Joe Jackson—did all right.

22. Maz, Quang, and Rudy

"*The only thing I ever wanted to do was to put one foot into the major leagues but they didn't want it. Now I can thank each and every veteran on the committee for allowing me to smell the roses. . . . I love baseball and today it looks like baseball loves me.*"

—Ray Dandridge, a Negro League veteran who near the end of his career got a shot with a Triple A farm club and performed well but was deemed too old to promote to the majors

Outside the cozy Bullpen Theater where he has just spoken to a packed crowd, John T. Bird signs copies of the book he wrote and published with one goal: to get his childhood hero into the Hall of Fame.

Bird grew up in Pennsylvania within walking distance of Pittsburgh's Forbes Field, a structure as tough as the city. There beside his father, a U.S. Steel attorney, in their seats behind third base, he cheered Clemente and Stargell and mere mortals like Gene Alley and Steve Blass. But the player he favored most was the second baseman, Bill Mazeroski, who in 1960 when Bird was a boy of five belted a last-of-the-ninth home run that defeated the Yankees and gave the Pirates their first world championship since 1925 and the days of Pie Traynor and Kiki Cuyler.

But it wasn't Mazeroski's October home run that enamored Bird. He marveled at how "Maz" played his position, how he pivoted at second base, how he got the ball from his mitt to his throwing hand in a blur, how he turned more double plays than anyone in history.

"Getting two outs with one pitch is really something," he says.

For fifteen years Bird watched in growing disgust as members of the Baseball Writers' Association of America elected other players to the Hall of Fame, thinking all along that they would promote Mazeroski in 1992, his final year on the writers' ballot. When instead they chose Tom Seaver and Rollie Fingers and rated Orlando Cepeda and Tony Perez higher, Bird flew into action.

"I thought he got the shaft," he says.

Players like Mazeroski who started their careers after 1945 and were named on at least one hundred ballots could be reconsidered for induction by the Veterans Committee. So Bird set out to bring attention to the feats of his hero. He wrote Mazeroski, telling him, "You deserve to be in the Hall of Fame." He asked that Mazeroski allow him to be his biographer. The player agreed, though doubtful that he belonged in Cooperstown.

Bird interviewed twenty-three former Pirates, wrote a book—*Twin Killing: The Bill Mazeroski Story*—and in 1995 published ten thousand copies at his own expense. Over the years he has given hundreds of copies to writers, broadcasters, former players, Veterans Committee members—anyone who could help the cause. He argued Mazeroski's case on a hundred radio shows and in numerous newspaper articles. He made a video of the infielder's career highlights. He persisted, even as others argued that with a .260 batting average Mazeroski didn't belong among baseball's best. "The basic problem that I saw was that the Hall of Fame was incomplete without the greatest fielder of all time," Bird says.

Last January the Veterans Committee met at the Tampa Airport Marriott and Bird went there to await the decision. When word leaked that Mazeroski, with crucial support from Hank Aaron, had been chosen, Bird took a fifty-minute taxi ride to Bradenton, Florida, where a celebration was underway.

Mazeroski, a warm but tough man who grew up poor in an Ohio coal-mining community, spotted Bird across the room. "Thank you! Thank you! Thank you!" he said, wrapping Bird in a hug.

"You made it on your own," Bird replied.

In fact it's never been that simple.

Traditionally, few ball players have gotten elected on the first ballot. It took Joe DiMaggio several tries, Dizzy Dean almost ten. That changed in the late 1970s. Now first-ballot elections have become common.

Some players have been hindered by poor relationships with writers, others by playing in small markets. If Bert Blyleven, for example, had collected most of his 287 victories with the New York Yankees rather than the Minnesota Twins, he would have been recognized by now. Similarly, those who play in the shadows of legends suffer.

That was the case with Harry Heilmann, who spent a dozen seasons as Ty Cobb's teammate. Heilmann led the league in hitting four times (with averages above .390) but didn't get into the Hall until his twelfth try—twenty years after he retired with a .342 career average.

When Heilmann was diagnosed with cancer in the spring of 1951, Ty Cobb began pushing behind the scenes. Cobb viewed his former teammate as second only to Rogers Hornsby among right-handed hitters. A respected sports writer of the time, Harry G. Salsinger, also wanted a special election to honor Heilmann before he died. "It will mean a great deal to him," Salsinger wrote in a letter to American League officials.

The Hall of Fame did not honor Heilmann until months after his death, but the fifty-six-year-old outfielder-turned-announcer passed away thinking he had joined the sport's immortals. While Heilmann was on his deathbed, his boyhood idol, Ty Cobb, told him he had been chosen for Cooperstown.

Author John T. Bird was insistent that nothing similar happen to Mazeroski. Though he declines credit for helping the Pirate attain the recognition, Bird is proud of the impact of his work on the star. "Before the book, Bill didn't think he should be in the Hall of Fame," says Bird. "After he read the book, he thought he belonged. It convinced him."

His mission complete, Bird intends to come for future inductions. But probably none will be sweeter than Sunday's.

At the information desk across from Bird, Quang Lam expects a similarly joyous experience this weekend. As a Hall of Fame intern he hopes to get a behind-the-scenes glimpse of the festivities and maybe to talk with George Brett, whose induction he witnessed in 1999.

"Brett has always been my favorite player," says Lam, a Royals fan since fifth grade.

Two years ago on an early Friday morning in late July, Lam

and a pair of college friends, Brandon and Vance, left Kansas City for Cooperstown in a rented Nissan Altima. They stopped in St. Louis to see Lam's sister and then headed east on the interstate traveling through Indianapolis and past Pittsburgh, arriving in Philadelphia the next morning. There was no game at Veterans Stadium, but they discovered that the Yankees were playing at home a mere hundred miles away. So they took off for New York City and watched Hideki Irabu and his teammates crush Cleveland, 21–1. Quang, Brandon, and Vance stayed in the city until 2 A.M. and then set out for Cooperstown. They arrived in the village about 7 A.M., secured a good spot for the ceremony, and slept for a few hours. "It was huge," he says. "There were people as far as I could see. We didn't know anybody." But they saw George Brett inducted with Nolan Ryan and Robin Yount. He and his friends stayed for Monday's Hall of Fame contest and even caught a game at Comiskey in Chicago on the trip home.

It's just one of Quang's many baseball adventures.

He also drove to St. Louis by himself in 1998 to watch Mark McGwire tie Roger Maris's record. He sat in left field. That same game, he won Tony LaRussa's jersey and got to go onto the diamond for the postgame presentation. He also witnessed McGwire's 67th, 68th, 69th, and 70th home runs.

A year ago while a volunteer at a Negro Leagues banquet, Quang ended up backstage with George Brett and Hank Aaron. Months earlier, hunting All-Star autographs at an Atlanta hotel, he overheard Dale Petroskey and struck up a conversation with the Hall of Fame president and learned about the internship program. Lam assists with the museum's Baseball Jeopardy game, the author series, and other activities.

Quang is a gregarious young man who looks younger than his twenty-four years. Within minutes of meeting him and hearing of his various road trips—he went to Montreal weeks ago and caught games in Baltimore and Philadelphia on the way there and back—I find myself offering to set him up with tickets when his baseball travels take him to Detroit.

But before he makes it to our city, he'll probably return to Vietnam where he was born. Quang, his older sister, and their father escaped the country after the war and after the communists took over. They were boat people, and they lived in a Malaysian refugee camp prior to making it to America. His mother and a younger brother followed two years later. Quang does not remember the ordeal or Vietnam. But he'd like to travel there.

I glance to see whether my brother is hearing this. He's not; he's with Dad, on a bench.

"Did Quang tell you he's a medical student?" asks a Hall of Fame employee.

"Huh?"

Quang took a leave from the University of Kansas, trying to decide whether he truly wants to become a physician. He hopes his Cooperstown summer will provide the answer.

Rudy Gafur pulls me into his world in less than ten seconds. "Kirby Puckett is a good man," he says. "But I don't think he should be going in on the first ballot. Eventually, yes. But not on the first ballot."

We're waiting near the museum's seven-foot, six hundred-pound statue of the cocky Mighty Casey—he for tickets to a private event, I for my nerves to settle. In a few minutes I will be speaking in the Bullpen Theater. They've already announced that fact twice over the museum public-address system, and visitors have begun to gather near the entrance. Though I've done numerous book talks, this marks my Cooperstown debut—and it feels more special than most.

You notice a couple things about Rudy immediately. He has a rich, pronounced West Indian accent, similar to the character Apu in the television show *The Simpsons*. Words roll from him in waves of genuine, unfettered enthusiasm.

"Cooperstown is my Mecca," he says, and he begins telling how he came to love baseball.

The story opens in what was British Guiana, a South American colony to which Rudy's forefathers were brought to labor on sugar plantations as indentured workers. The country, now Guyana, has a tropical climate and is lush and rich in waterfalls. Rudy grew up there during the 1940s and 1950s, learning soccer and cricket.

"British Guiana did not have baseball," he says. "But I knew there was a player named Babe Ruth because the whole world knew that, and I knew there was a Roy Campanella. I had seen him in a magazine bubble gum ad."

In 1972, six years after Guyana gained its independence from Britain, Gafur immigrated to Canada with his wife and five children. Five springs later during the inaugural season of the Toronto Blue Jays, he saw his first game. It snowed. "I was so preoccupied with staying warm I did not know what was going on."

A university administrator, Gafur thought a trip to the ballpark would be an ideal activity for freshman orientation. So he arranged for five hundred students to go. The game piqued his interest. By 1984 he was hooked, attending almost every Blue Jays home contest. When the team was on the road, he listened to Tony Kubek and frequently heard the announcer mention Ty Cobb. "I became fascinated with this Ty Cobb," he says.

Rudy went to Cooperstown for the first time in the summer of 1986. "I was in wonderland. As a little boy I had read James Fenimore Cooper's *Leatherstocking Tales*. It was beyond my wildest dreams that someday I would be here. I went with a purpose. I wanted to see Lake Glimmerglass—Otsego Lake. I wanted to see the Susquehanna River. I wanted to see Council Rock. They were all here. After two hundred years this place is almost unspoiled."

He has come back every year since. "Some years I've come three times. I love the place so damn much." On one visit he got to know Ty Cobb's youngest son, Jim. They became friends and Jim Cobb painted a picture of his father that balanced the common portrait of Cobb as a bitter, mean racist.

"As a colored person I should dislike Ty Cobb," Gafur says. "But I do not. While I do not condone his bigotry, I can explain it. I judge him by the time in which he lived. I judge the players on the basis of what they do between the white lines."

Rudy drives to Cooperstown. It takes him a leisurely five hours from his Toronto-area home. "I have never gone alone," he says. This year he came with a man he met summers earlier. "He's a human being and a baseball fan. We have so much in common. You can't go wrong."

Gafur, who is sixty, knows dozens of fans who come annually for the big weekend. He has made friends. "People say, 'Why do you go every year?' You have to go to experience the passion of the people. It's no wonder baseball is called the national pastime."

His enthusiasm led him to publish a book in 1995 titled *Cooperstown Is My Mecca*. Ask him to tell you of his highlights and, though he can draw from a vast collection of colorful anecdotes involving the most famous of ball players, he chooses two humble, soft-focus moments from the 1980s.

The first took place in Cooper Park outside the museum where the ceremony used to be held. A limo pulled up and an elderly black man emerged in suit and cap. He was frail, blind in one eye, and nearly blind in the other. But when a Hall of Fame attendant offered help he declined. Rudy recognized him as a Negro Leagues legend and took it upon himself to introduce the eighty-four-year-old. "I said, 'Folks, we are lucky to have among us Cool Papa Bell.' Everybody stood beside him at a respectful distance. Bell wanted to savor the moment. Here he was at the seat of baseball, the repository, The Shrine." Cool Papa Bell had once been proclaimed the fastest man to ever run the bases, and here he was walking slowly on the sidewalk, every precarious step braced by a cane. The irony struck Rudy.

The second moment occurred outside the Otesaga Hotel, where fans used to arrive early for a chance to have Hall of Famers sign autographs. Rudy had been waiting for hours, but as he approached Happy Chandler, who was almost ninety, a waiter brought Chandler his breakfast: a cup of tea and two slices of toast. Chandler, who had been commissioner when

Jackie Robinson came to the majors, was seated next to "Catfish" Hunter. "Everyone waited as he broke his toast into tiny pieces and soaked them in his tea before eating, just as a child would." The sight reminded Rudy of the adage "Once a man, twice a child."

"This place gives me an opportunity to experience vicariously what guys like you saw growing up," Rudy says. "When I see Enos Slaughter, I don't see a shrinking old man. I see a man charging from first to score on a double in the 1946 World Series. When I see the Splendid Splinter on the street, I see a young kid, Ted Williams."

23. September 1972: Campy's Flying Bat

Mom returned home from the hospital the same week that Yogi Berra, Sandy Koufax, and six others got enshrined in New York.

"The Hall of Fame induction ceremony was baseball drama at its best," reported the Associated Press. The article recounted how Berra teared up remembering his late parents and how Koufax humbly admitted that after his first five seasons in the majors he thought his career nearly over. The journalist described a pastoral scene outside the hall where thousands witnessed the enshrinement. It was an historic day, he said.

I showed the story to my dad. I'm not sure why—maybe just to share it and get him talking baseball, maybe to see if he had

---

ABOVE: Mickey Lolich and Billy Martin *(Detroit Public Library, Burton Historical Collection)*

changed his mind, to test whether there was some glimmer of hope of us still going, or maybe to make him feel guilty for depriving me of my dream.

He studied the photo that accompanied the article. It pictured Berra and Koufax with fellow living inductees Lefty Gomez, Buck Leonard, and Early Wynn.

Gomez, who pitched for the Yankees when Dad was a boy, had been credited with nicknaming Charlie Gehringer "The Mechanical Man."

"Old Lefty sure had to wait a long time for Cooperstown," Dad said.

I wondered how long I would have to wait.

B y week's end the Baltimore Orioles had leapt past the Tigers into first place.

Billy Martin dictated a message to Earl Weaver. "Tell him we'll be back," he said. "Tell him it's temporary and don't get used to it." But after four straight losses, Martin grew so frustrated with his team's poor hitting that he picked his batting order from a hat. Slow-footed slugger Norm Cash, who hadn't stolen a base all year, hit leadoff, and Eddie Brinkman, usually eighth, anchored the cleanup position. Willie Horton homered and Detroit won 3-2.

The Tigers had acquired Woodie Fryman, a Kentucky tobacco farmer, from the Phillies in early August and then catcher Duke Sims from the Dodgers. Woodie and Duke. They sounded like cowboy heroes who had ridden in from the West to save the franchise. Their stats, though, promised no such thing. Fryman had a lousy record and a sore left arm, and Sims was hitting worse than Brinkman. Even a boy delirious with home-team fever couldn't imagine the roles they would play.

When Bill Freehan got injured, Sims became the starting catcher and promptly began knocking in game-winning runs. He raised his average to over .300. "I need a job next year," he explained. "They don't remember what you do in April or May but they remember the things you did to help late in the season."

Fryman debuted as a Detroit starter by shutting out the Yankees and Mel Stottlemyre. Next, he defeated Gaylord Perry and then Gaylord's older brother, Jim. It took "Catfish" Hunter to hand Fryman his first loss. Woodie was averaging a run-and-a-half per game. "I know my arm can fall off any time I pitch but I'll keep on pitching until it does," he said. "I've just got to live with it."

Fryman didn't falter. In September he beat the Indians, the Orioles, and the Brewers—each two times. After Detroit dropped to a season-low fourth place on September 11, Fryman set things right. And in the final week of the strike-shortened regular season, with the Tigers behind Boston, Fryman ignited a five-game winning streak. Then, before 51,500 hometown fans, Mickey Lolich ousted John Curtis and the Red Sox from first place. The next day Fryman clinched the division title by four-hitting the Sox and besting Luis Tiant, who had been on a torrid roll of his own. Fryman raised his Detroit record to 10-3.

"He's pitching like Schoolboy Rowe," Dad said.

Lynwood Thomas Rowe, son of a circus trapeze performer,

rose to the majors in 1933. Manager Mickey Cochrane declared him faster than Lefty Grove. Rowe was twenty-one, a six-foot-four Arkansas farm boy loaded with charisma and talent. "What will baseball do for a blazing spot of color when Babe Ruth retires?" wondered *New York World-Telegram* columnist C. E. Parker. "If there is a Ruthian figure on the horizon, Schoolboy Rowe is the feller."

Like Ruth, a pitcher early in his career, Rowe could hit. In his second season, he batted .303 in 109 attempts and brought in 22 runs. But he amazed fans with his performance on the mound. Rowe won sixteen straight, tying a record held by Grove, Walter Johnson, and Joe Wood. His sterling performance led the team past the Yankees and into the World Series against the Cardinals. Dad was fourteen.

Sport magazine carried a feature in September titled "Mickey Lolich and the Pride Within." It told how Lolich had long been overlooked, first playing in Denny McLain's shadow and then having his brilliant 1971 season eclipsed by Vida Blue. "All my life it's been the other guys who were heroes while I just plugged along and tried to do my job," he said. "I know my name will be forgotten two years after I take Detroit off my shirt."

Lolich opened the American League playoff series against "Catfish" Hunter in Oakland on a Saturday in early October. It felt like football weather in Detroit. We ate chili in front of the television, me crumbling crackers into mine, Dad shaking ketchup into his.

It wasn't long before I had started in about Lolich and his Hall of Fame potential. He had, after all, finished the regular season with 22 wins, fourth best in the majors behind Steve Carlton, Gaylord Perry, and Wilbur Wood. He had won more than twenty in two consecutive seasons. "Maybe he'll win three more World Series games," I said.

"Well, he knows how to win the big ones. I'll give him that," Dad said.

Al Kaline, thirty-seven, had been on a hitting tear in the final weeks of the season, driving in the run that secured the division title.

Kaline was good in the clutch, like little Tommy Bridges, Dad said.

Bridges played sixteen seasons in Detroit and appeared in four World Series. One baseball columnist long ago described him this way: "He isn't any bigger than a minute . . . and looks like a stand-in for Mahatma Gandhi." In the 1934 Series, Bridges put his club ahead three games to two in a pitching duel with Dizzy Dean. A year later he brought the city its first championship, beating the Cubs in Game Six. It was tied 3-3 in the ninth when Stan Hack tripled to deep center with no one out. Bridges bore down, fanning Bill Jurges on three pitches. He got Larry French to dribble a two-strike pitch back to the mound, and then enticed Augie Galan to end the inning on an easy fly to left. The adrenaline carried the team to victory. In the locker room, manager Mickey Cochrane praised Bridges. "Just look at him," he told Gehringer, Greenberg, and the others. "Just look at him and feel proud you were ever on the same team with him. He's a hundred and fifty pounds of sheer guts."

If anything could have erase my disappointment over not going to Cooperstown, it would have been a trip to the World Series for the Tiger team in which I invested my heart that summer. The whole 1972 season had been building toward it. We had made the playoffs, as Billy Martin had predicted. In the first game, Dad and I watched the Tigers take an early lead. The A's tied it soon afterward, and the game remained knotted into the 11th inning. With Lolich still pitching, Kaline homered and it looked as if our team would be two victories away from the World Series.

But the celebration lasted only minutes. Oakland rallied, and in an astonishing change of fortune, the A's won on a rare wild throw by Kaline. "I never went from being a hero to a goat any quicker in my whole life," he said.

Sunday afternoon Dad and I were in front of the television for Game Two, with Woodie Fryman facing John "Blue Moon" Odom. Joey popped into the living room to check the score before leaving the house. Oakland had added to its lead in the fifth. The A's were up 4-0 when reliever Lerrin LaGrow pelted Bert Campaneris on the ankle. Campaneris retaliated by hurling his bat at LaGrow. The pitcher ducked as the Louisville Slugger twirled over his head toward second base. The benches emptied, and the umpires restrained Billy Martin.

"That's the dirtiest thing I ever saw in my whole life in baseball," said Martin, denying that he had ordered LaGrow to throw at Campaneris.

By Tuesday the Tigers were down two games to none and on the verge of elimination. The only thing kids at school talked about that day was Bert Campaneris, how he ought to be tossed out of baseball, how Willie Horton could punish him with his fists, how the Tigers had to win now.

That afternoon the school counselor interrupted art class and asked if she could borrow me for a few minutes. We had talked before. I liked Mrs. Ballenger. She had golden brown hair that curled above her shoulders. Her eyes looked soft and bright. She enjoyed being with junior high kids, which, odd as it may seem, wasn't the impression all teachers gave. We sat in her small office, down the hall from the assistant principal's chamber of torture, and she asked how I was doing and how Mom was feeling and how that made me feel and whether I thought Mom's illness might be affecting my grades or if I knew of some other reason that I had been getting into trouble because it was so unlike me and she realized I was a good kid. When we had finished, she escorted me back to class, her arm on my shoulder.

"By the way," she said, "the Tigers are winning."

It occurred to me on the walk home, listening on a portable radio as Joe Coleman struck out the A's, that I had been jinxing the Tigers by watching on television. It was my fault they had lost two in a row. As a fan you needed to be aware of such things. You needed to be sensitive to how your seemingly innocent actions could sabotage an entire season. In a close game you could never be sure what might alter the fickle winds of fortune. So I stayed on the cement porch in front of the house and listened to Ernie Harwell. And it worked. The Tigers won 3-0.

I did the same on Wednesday, and they won again. Down

by two, the Tigers rallied in the tenth inning. I was under the birch tree on the front lawn when Jim Northrup sent the series into a fifth and final game. The Tigers would face "Blue Moon" Odom, who had accused Billy Martin of targeting Campaneris. "It will be Woodie Fryman pitching for us," said Martin, "and 'Mouthy' going for them. . . . We've got all the exits cut off. . . . There's no way he can escape."

Melby Junior High released its students earlier than Frost Elementary, which meant I beat Jeff Mancini home most days by about twenty minutes. By the time I got out of school on Thursday, Oakland was in front 2-1. Woodie Fryman was still pitching; Odom had left the game for Vida Blue. I waited outside Frost, wanting to be the first to tell Jeff the good news that was to come.

Jim Northrup got on base in the seventh, Willie Horton in the eighth, and Norm Cash in the ninth and each time it seemed as if the Tigers were about to pull ahead. But the rally never materialized, and when the game ended I felt stunned and surprised that someone else's heroes would be playing Johnny Bench in the World Series.

Bench had hit eleven home runs that September, cementing his MVP. But in the World Series, it was another catcher, Gene Tenace, who dominated the headlines, belting four of five Oakland round-trippers, knocking in more than half of the A's runs, bringing home the winning run in two games, and scoring it in another. The Oakland A's surprised Cincinnati and Jimmy the Greek by winning it all.

That autumn Jeff Mancini and I drifted apart. Over the years our friendship had suffered through the usual childhood jealousies and disagreements and wrongs, some perceived, some real, but it had always endured, even after our disputes spiraled into physical battles. Rather than end in flames, our friendship gradually dissolved as each of us found other friends who in their newness appeared more interesting. We played together on the St. Malachy team for another two seasons, even teamed up in an all-star game at second and short. But it was different by then, so much so that when Jeff moved in 1974 neither of us bothered to stay in touch.

Mom's August surgery failed to heal. The incision festered, and an ugly pus oozed from under a tapestry of scab and shiny pink skin. Her ordeal was far from over. A few weeks after Roberto Clemente's plane disappeared into the Atlantic Ocean on New Year's Eve, Mom returned to the hospital, facing the first of several more operations. They cut two ribs from her chest and placed them in her skull.

It had become apparent in late 1972 that the military draft would end before Joey would be called to fight. The head of the armed services had announced his plan to finish the draft early. I learned something about my brother then. His strong feelings against the war didn't depend on the threat that he would have to serve. That issue aside, he continued to speak against it.

I n August 1973, in the days before he got married, my brother prepared to move from the house on Shawn Drive.

He emptied the clothes from his dresser and cleared out his art supplies. He stacked his albums and eight-track tapes in milk crates and he slid his rolled Woodstock posters into tubes.

The ghosts of them remained on the faded walls, their shapes in brilliant yellow.

I was sitting on his bed, beneath a hanging lamp with a black-light bulb, watching him fill cardboard boxes. Rod Stewart was singing about "Gasoline Alley."

"You should get some cool baseball stuff and decorate the room," Joey said.

Shortly, his room would be mine and the Kaline and Bench posters would go up and maybe Dad would install one of those bat racks that were available by mail order in the back of baseball magazines.

"You should be excited about getting your own space, Tommy. I didn't get my own room until I was fourteen. You'll like the privacy. It's a big step."

It was a big step but not nearly as big as his. He was moving into an apartment, not just a different room. It was like that no matter how old I got, no matter what new privileges came my way. He remained seven steps ahead of me, and I would never catch up. I'd never hang out with him and his friends, I'd never play fast pitch with him (not that he played much anymore). I felt destined to remain his kid brother, forever a boy in his eyes.

I realized then—in the way that twelve-year-olds realize things—that my life would be changing irrevocably. Joey would be leaving for good, heading off into a life separate from mine. I was gaining a room and losing my brother. It wasn't nearly as good as the Norm Cash trade.

Joey had cleared out most of the room. All that remained was the closet, and there wasn't much left in it. We packed a souvenir steel drum, a train set, a tattered copy of *Bury My*

Heart at Wounded Knee, and much more under the basement steps. We carried some boxes to the car and stacked others in the hallway. All that remained was a pile of papers and publications.

He flipped through them, studied me for a moment, arched his eyebrows above the top of his wire-rim glasses, and gave me his goofy look. "You can sort through these later," he said. "Maybe there's something you want to keep."

After he left I sifted through the stack. It was a gold mine. There were programs from Detroit Lions games that he had attended with his future father-in-law. There were Red Wings, Pistons, and Tigers yearbooks and scorecards and newspapers.

But between them were three thick magazines.

He must not have seen them. He couldn't have meant to leave them for me. It had to be an accident. It was an accident, right? He didn't really think I should have these, did he? Mom would kill him if she found out. She would kill *me.* On one of the covers was a woman in bubbles; on another, a woman in fur; and on the third, a woman whose face I could not see but whose top button was undone on her jeans and whose shirt was lifted part way up. They were wearing way too little clothes.

PLAYBOY MAGAZINE, the cover proclaimed. ENTERTAINMENT FOR MEN.

24. Babe Ruth Day

Al *Kaline's "voice cracked and as he talked
about his debt to his parents, who were there, I
got a little tear in my eye, too, like everyone else.
The horrible thought occurred to me, 'If this
happens while I'm listening to Al talk about his
parents, what's going to happen to me when I
get up there?' I sort of looked toward the sky
and said silently, 'Mom and Dad, I'm not going
to talk too much about you today.' I'm sure
they understood. . . ."*

—Duke Snider recalling his 1980 induction in
The Duke of Flatbush

Ready?" asks Bruce Markusen.

Markusen, the voice of Hall of Fame programs and productions, accompanies me into the Bullpen Theater. He and I share a devotion to early 1970s baseball, and knowing my affection for the Tigers of 1972 he has brought his collection of Topps cards from that year. "I'm missing Les Cain," he says.

A memory flickers of my brother in the garage on Shawn Drive. It's a hot, late-summer night, probably August of 1970. He's sixteen, I'm nine, and we're playing ball with his friends. Actually I'm in the driveway on the fringe of their fun, pretending to be part of the action. Mom's silver convertible and Dad's banana-yellow Camaro (both purchased before the surgeries began) are gone. Joey has flipped on the garage light and in its uneven glow is whipping a rubber ball against the drywall as his buddies take turns swinging. When they connect, they sometimes line the ball through the garage toward the street. More often it ricochets off a bench or the lawn mower or a half-can of avocado paint—anywhere, we all hope, but off the two bulbs in the ceiling socket that allow our game to be under the lights. Pretending to be Les Cain, Joey hammers the wall with a pitch. It leaves a round smudge mark. It's a strike.

"Shhhhugarrrrr Cain," he says triumphantly. It sounds cool the way he growls the words.

For the next week, I mimic him. "Shhhhugarrrrr Cain . . . Shhhhugarrrrr Cain . . . Shhhhugarrrrr Cain."

Les "Sugar" Cain showed promise in 1970, winning twelve games in what would be his best season. Two years later Billy Martin looked to Cain as his fourth starter but the pitcher floundered. "I don't know what Cain's problem is," said Martin. "But I know I'm going to have to find out." That season marked Cain's last. Arm trouble finished his modest career.

There's nothing specific for which I remember Les Cain, save for that one night. But it's amazing how a missing baseball card can take me back there.

Les Cain has faded into the footnotes with thousands of other men who played bit roles in the major leagues, men mostly forgotten except by the Bruce Markusens of the world. Those lesser-known players illustrate one of baseball's—and life's—most basic truths: We can't all be stars. We can't all be Kalines and Clementes and Henry Aarons. But we can all play roles.

Remember the world champion Oakland A's of 1972? Reggie Jackson. Sal Bando. "Catfish" Hunter. Joe Rudi. Rollie Fingers.

You know the names. They and others held the spotlight. But a cast of forty-seven men—from Adrian Garrett and "Downtown" Ollie Brown to Tim Cullen and Angel Mangual—appeared with Oakland that season, contributing in various ways. (Well, maybe not Garrett, who went hitless in eleven at bats.)

"I loved reading the transactions column back then," says Markusen, an expert on the A's dynasty. "Charlie Finley had a revolving door. He tinkered."

Markusen lived in New York as a boy but rooted for Oakland, initially intrigued by the green polyester uniforms. It was his favorite color. "You latch on to a team for strange reasons," he says. A Yankee fan by birth, Markusen has authored several books on icons from the early 1970s. One features his hero, Roberto Clemente. Markusen is half Puerto Rican. His late mother, Ana Graciela, came from Santurce, Puerto Rico, where Clemente debuted professionally.

"There's a tendency to say baseball was in its golden era in the 1950s," he says. "In New York it certainly was. But in the 1970s it wasn't the New York teams dominating. You had all these other teams winning: Baltimore, Oakland, Pittsburgh, Cincinnati, Los Angeles. I gravitate nostalgically to that era. It's an underrated time in baseball history."

D ale Petroskey introduces me to the fifty or so people who have gathered in the Bullpen Theater to hear about the last summer at Tiger Stadium. I was offered the honor of coming to the Hall of Fame today to discuss my book *The Final Season*. The invitation provided the perfect reason to visit Cooperstown. Otherwise our trip might never have happened. We would have continued talking about how someday we should go to the Hall of Fame until too many somedays had slipped past us.

The last year at Tiger Stadium I went to all 81 home games to say goodbye to a place I knew well. Four generations of my family had shared the sport there over much of nine decades, from my grandfather to my father, to my brother and me, to our children. Even someone who doesn't care for baseball can understand what compels the spirit to embrace such a place. We made memories there. We came to know it intimately. It connected us. It was much like the family home in that respect, harbored in our hearts.

But what of this Hall of Fame? Many visitors see it only once. It's not a place we know in the physical sense. It's not a building to which we've developed an attachment. We've made no memories here, not most of us anyway. So why do we come, and why does it touch us so?

Cooperstown is all about anticipation—the anticipation of going, the anticipation of being inducted. You begin dreaming as a child for something that won't be fulfilled—if ever—until you've played at least ten years and been retired for at least five. Even if you've been lucky enough to play in the major leagues and good enough to have excelled, there are no guarantees. The wait haunts former ball players as they drift into the autumns of their lives, pretending in their interviews that they've dispensed of those hopes, saying they don't ever expect to make it, perhaps believing it but still wondering when it gets that time of year and the ballots go out and the Veterans Committee meets, wondering if maybe it will finally happen.

After I finish telling the Cooperstown audience about Tiger

Stadium—with my dad watching from the back row and my brother off to my left standing near the doorway taking photos, their presence making me less nervous—other baseball fans share their stories, of trips to ball fields, of fathers and sons and daughters, of baseball memories.

There's a stereotype that paints men as emotionally distant, and I once accepted it as true. But no more. Everything I've witnessed over the past twenty years contradicts that tired notion. I've seen men as they celebrate their daughters' diplomas, as they leave familiar jobs for new ones, as they hold babies at christenings, reminisce about their grandmothers' popcorn balls, and linger in the sniffling darkness of movie theaters. I've seen World War II soldiers saluting during the playing of "Taps" on Memorial Day and baseball fans at the final game in a dying ballpark. I've heard my stoic Uncle George when his dog Pepper died and I've listened to a friend tell how he cares for his sickly father every day after work. Almost always it's about family or friends and joy or loss. Those emotions lie near the surface for many who come to Cooperstown because the place brings forth days long past and the people who colored them.

In the front row, there's a guy in his late fifties, a solid, sturdy, big-shouldered man, masculine, confident. He begins beaming about the ballpark of his lifetime and the day his grandfather took him to Yankee Stadium. It was June 13, 1948, and he was a young boy. It was Babe Ruth Day, the Bambino's last appearance at the park, and the Yankees were retiring his number. You've no doubt seen the Pulitzer Prize–winning picture that captured the moment: The Babe, still as a statue, his back to the camera, shoulders slightly slumped, head almost bowed, his cap in his left hand at his side, his bat a crutch, the crowd a blur in the stands, the world champion banners hanging from the roof in right.

"I didn't understand the significance of the day," the man begins. "But my grandfather . . ." And then he stops abruptly as his voice cracks, as if he's just now realizing that his grandfather's gone and Ruth's gone and maybe his father, too, and that Yankee Stadium doesn't look the same and half a century has disappeared and he's now a man, a father, maybe a grandfather himself, and it's all starting to make sense to him, the bittersweetness of the moment. He misses some of his past, treasures his now, and in his maturity sees the beauty in the gift of the grandfather who must have realized that the boy would remember little of that day but took him anyway, thinking it might mean something decades later. Could he have known that his grandson would think of him whenever he heard the name Babe Ruth?

The man waits for his knotted throat to relax. "I'm sorry," he says, "my grandfather . . . my grandfather wanted me to see Babe Ruth."

When the Hall of Fame opened in 1939, it was a gala affair that crowded the streets of the village and brought to town all eleven living inductees. The group photo shows only ten because Ty Cobb arrived late, some say to avoid Judge Kenesaw Mountain Landis. They're all in coats and ties, except for

Ruth, who has an open collar and is sitting in the front row, his legs crossed, his socks rolled down, his bare legs showing beneath cuffed pants. There's Connie Mack next to him, straight as a board, and Cy Young, with pipe in hand, staring off in the distance at something other than the camera, and Grover Cleveland Alexander, his dark hair slicked back, looking like a Southern preacher.

The dedication took place on the false centennial of baseball's birth. That first year—over the entire calendar year—25,000 fans came to the town. Not until after World War II did annual attendance top that level and then it escalated quickly to 93,000 in 1949, the summer after Ruth died. In the years of Mantle, Mays, and Aaron, the figure crept gradually toward 200,000, a plateau first topped in 1971. Another sixteen seasons passed before it reached 300,000 and then in 1989, the year Bench and Yastrzemski were enshrined, it topped 400,000, its highest total to date.

Certainly better roads and promotional efforts have contributed to the Hall of Fame's growth. But something more is at work.

In 1994 when the Hall of Fame was undergoing improvements, a custodian found a black-and-white photograph where a World War II exhibit had been. It featured an anonymous player in a 1940s Sinclair Oil industrial-league uniform. On the back was this note: "You were never too tired to play catch. On your days off you helped build the Little League field. You always came to watch me play. You were a Hall of Fame dad. I wish I could share this moment with you. Your son, Pat."

The find drew national publicity. A journalist discovered

that the photo had been left by a man who lived in western New York. More than three decades after his father's death, with no fanfare, the man slipped the picture beneath a display case.

After the renovations, museum curator Ted Spencer returned the photo to the area where the son had left it. Spencer said it would serve as a tribute to all fathers who passed the game onto their children.

With each season that distances us from our childhood, with each year that claims more of our fathers and mothers, with every vintage ballpark that must give way to a shiny new palace that our grandfathers didn't visit, the Hall of Fame takes on deeper significance. People certainly come to celebrate the sport, but more than that they come to celebrate family and friends. They come to touch memories that few other places can evoke.

25. The Old Guy in the Big Glasses

"I'd like to say thanks to my father who isn't here today . . . my brother Richard who caught me between houses, in the alley, and on the playing field . . . to Detroit, too, for allowing me to use their sandlot playgrounds where I played with my first team, the All-City Stars, and then on to an excellent American Legion program with Roose-Vanker Post 286 where I was picked up by Wish Egan, a scout for Detroit."

—Harold "Prince Hal" Newhouser at his induction

Last night in the Hall of Fame gallery, a boy of about ten in a Nomar Garciaparra jersey was gazing at the grinning, bronzed image of Willie Mays. The boy lifted his right hand toward the plaque, cautious, as if Mays might speak to him and warn him off. He slid his fingers over the raised letters that spelled out "The Say Hey Kid." Mays would have been sixty when the boy was born.

Down a bit, Dad had located Hal Newhouser in an alcove between Rollie Fingers and Reggie Jackson, among a group of players inducted in the early 1990s. He stood before Newhouser's plaque, his mouth open—though not in awe—his right fist clenched and propped on his hip. "Only pitcher in major-league history to win back-to-back MVP awards," the plaque states. "Strikeout king with blazing fastball."

"You remembering the time you broke up Newhouser's no-hitter?" I asked. I said the words loudly so he would hear them—and maybe so others would hear them as well. My voice carried through the gallery.

The boy in the Red Sox jersey snapped his eyes in our direction, wondering who the old guy in the big glasses might be. He darted from Willie Mays to his own father and told him in a voice that defied his whisper, "That guy used to play baseball." They studied my father, who was unaware of the attention.

"Oh, he was a competitor," Dad said. "Newhouser hated to lose. He'd get peeved at his teammates if they muffed a play. He'd give them a nasty look and slap his glove."

Dad contorted his face into a snarl, impersonating a perturbed, aged Newhouser.

"Boy, could he throw hard."

Dad went silent for a moment.

It's 1938 at Georgia Park near City Airport on Detroit's east side, on the grounds of Burrough Middle School, in the shadow of St. Cyril Church, not far from the streetcar tracks along Van Dyke Avenue, on a sandy infield on an afternoon in spring, sparrows flitting in elm trees, squirrels scrambling along branches, Grandpa Stankiewicz—today forty-four years dead—smoking a cigar and watching from the wooden stands.

Dad is eighteen, and he and his Federation League teammates have swaggered over to the next field and challenged the defending American Legion state champions, Roose-Vanker, to an impromptu scrimmage. Their buddy, Jimmy Reggio, plays for the Legion team, which is known throughout the area. It stars seventeen-year-old Harold Newhouser, who made headlines the year prior by striking out twenty-four batters in one game and throwing a no-hitter in the state tournament. He has grown taller over the winter and looks formidable on the mound.

A temperamental lefty, Newhouser has a fiery fastball and a streak of wildness. The combination intimidates batters. Dad and his pals soon realize they are outmatched. Newhouser blows through their lineup, striking them out at will, barely surrendering a foul ball—until my dad, protecting the plate on a two-strike pitch, swings late and drops a hit over the first baseman's head. The ball careens out of play for a double. Newhouser glares at the first baseman and the right fielder, his disgust implying that both might have caught the ball if only they had tried.

Three innings later he faces my dad a second time.

"He looks like he wants to kill me."

The first pitch scorches the edge of the batter's box, inches inside the plate. The next two hit the outside corner. The count at one ball, two strikes, Dad reaches for the fourth pitch. It scuffs the end of his bat and drops along the right-field line. Again, it rolls for a double.

"That was foul," Newhouser argues. He points and stammers and whacks his glove against his leg. The umpire does not relent.

Dad waits on second. Newhouser steps off the mound, turns from home plate, and glowers at my father, his hands on his hips, his head shaking in disrespect.

"I never did score," Dad said. "He struck out almost everybody."

Newhouser won, of course. But Joseph Stankiewicz got the only hits he surrendered that afternoon. Two doubles. It seemed logical to Dad that if people were talking about Newhouser going pro, they might also consider the second baseman who had crushed his no-hitter, perhaps the only man in the world to have a .667 career average against the future Hall of Famer.

The next year Newhouser entered the minor leagues in Texas. By September the Tigers had called him north. He debuted that autumn after his senior year, playing with Gehringer and Greenberg and the other stars whose ball cards Dad had saved.

"Newhouser used to drive into our neighborhood and show off his car," Dad said. "I don't remember the make but it was red. A red car. I remember that."

For a while Dad resented him.

"I figured if I had gotten the break, I'd be with the Tigers playing with Gehringer. I wondered why I wasn't picked up. Then I started convincing myself that the minor leaguers didn't get much money and that I wouldn't have signed even if they had offered me a contract and then World War II came."

"You wouldn't have signed?"

"Maybe," he said.

Dad followed the Tigers and Newhouser in the papers while stationed in Missouri. When Prince Hal, as he had become known, stormed through the 1944 season toward 29 victories, Dad told his pals at the NCO club how he had faced him when both were prospects. Sometimes they believed him. As the pitcher garnered All-Star honors and twenty-win seasons, Dad grew increasingly proud. "Well, I did play against him," he said. "At the same level."

Standing before Newhouser's plaque Dad felt a tingle course up his spine. "Part of me knows I wasn't good enough to make it here," he said. "But another part of me will always wonder."

My dad, maybe like yours, has spent much of his life in the shadows, working the usual shifts and sometimes Saturdays in a job that brought no glory but paid the bills. You never read about him in the papers or heard about him on television and about the most he ever got in the way of awards were some certificates from his employer and a bowling trophy or two. But he gave me and my brother and our sisters a childhood empty of horrors. There are no beatings or drunken episodes, no neglect or abuse, in our past. Mine was an ordinary suburban childhood with charcoal barbeques, picnics and baseball, Scout meetings, household chores, games of catch, two weeks' vacation in summer, a not-quite-new car in the garage, a good share of sweet moments, and a few memorable disappointments.

How you view your father changes over time. He starts as Superman and in adolescence evolves into Gomer Pyle. Eventually, if you've had a good life, you come to appreciate him and, later still, begin recognizing yourself in your memories of the man.

When I was a boy we used to get up early on Sunday mornings and he'd drive my sister and me to Detroit. He'd take us to Belle Isle, an island park where he spent many hours as a teen and occasionally slept with his brothers under the stars on hot nights. He'd show us the fountain where he brought Mom on her first trip north. He'd point to the canals on which he once canoed and he'd escort us through the small aquarium with its cavelike walls and into the humid botanical garden and past the once-glorious casino. We'd leave the island and he'd drive the lonesome downtown streets, noting the Faygo pop plant, the twenty-five-story Hudson's building, the Wonder Bread factory, the docked Boblo steamer, and the Ambassador Bridge that linked the city to Windsor, Ontario. He'd cruise by the empty sports landmarks: Cobo Arena where Dave Bing and the Pistons played; Olympia Stadium, home to Gordie Howe and the Red Wings; and Tiger Stadium, the best of them all. This was in the years after the race riots. Many buildings remained boarded and the streets were desolate on weekend mornings. Detroit had become known for murder and crime. But in the car with Dad we felt safe and protected as if no harm could pierce his armor.

He was—is—a Mickey Lolich father: dependable, consistent, capable, seldom flashy, successful more often than not, a workhorse not a racehorse. I'll admit that there were times I wanted an Al Kaline dad, someone who did something more exciting than work in a darkroom at a tank plant.

There is a portrait of Kaline and his family in the 1972 Tigers yearbook. The four of them are seated in the dugout. Al has on his Tiger uniform, his cap in his lap and his left arm stretched across the back of the bench, reaching to his wife Louise's shoulder. She looks like a model in an open-collared

blue-check dress, her hair coiffed and curled. Their blond sons
sit between them, Mark in a Detroit uniform, Mike wearing his
dad's glove. All four are smiling like their world is perfect and
there's no place they'd rather be. There's another photo of Kaline, this one taken in an airport. He's perched on luggage between Mickey Stanley and Jim Northrup, and they look sharp
in their wide-lapel sports coats and shiny striped ties, Kaline in
stylish boot shoes and Northrup and Stanley in snazzy white
bucks.

My dad looked nothing like Kaline or Northrup or Stanley
or the men in the ads in the sports magazines, the guys with
thick wavy hair, full mustaches, and flared Hagar slacks. In the
stretch of years when Mom was sick and money was tight, he
wore stained work shirts and snagged polyester-blend pants.

"Why don't you get some cool clothes?" I asked him once.
It wasn't really a question.

For Christmases and birthdays, he requested the same boring items: black socks and white underwear—gifts no kid
wanted to receive (or bestow). It never occurred to us that he
might actually need them. Now we buy him shirts and pants
and sweatshirts and ball caps and he has more than he can
possibly wear.

I was out of high school when his friend Jack Stanfield
stopped by the house one afternoon, which was unusual. Jack
usually dropped in on Friday or Saturday nights with his drinking buddy, Al, another of Dad's coworkers. If he had recently
been back home near Jellico, Kentucky, Jack might have a jug
of moonshine with him. He and Al would often be "two sheets
to the wind," in Dad's words, and they would get sillier as they

got drunker. (I have a picture of Colleen and me sitting in a playpen with Al and a menagerie of stuffed animals; he has a blue bear on his head.)

Jack wasn't drunk the afternoon he rolled into our driveway in his Cadillac Fleetwood. He had come looking for my dad but found me instead. We ended up talking for a half hour about how Jack had come to Detroit poor, literally arriving barefoot, standing on the sidewalk and looking up in amazement at the skyscrapers. As an adult Jack was six-three, loud and brash, unforgiving to those who did him wrong but absolutely faithful to friends like my dad. If you didn't know him—or even if you did—he might scare you off.

"I ain't nothing but a hillbilly, Tommy, but I know something about people. And I'll tell you this: There's a lot of assholes in this world but your dad ain't one of them. He's the goddamn nicest man I know and there ain't nothing I wouldn't do for him. I ain't bullshitting you, Tommy. He's the best man I know, goddamnit."

If that had been the only time I heard such praise, it might never have stuck. But other longtime friends and relatives said the same thing. My mother told me that, too—on the day she announced they would be divorcing. "Your dad is the nicest man I know," she said, her eyes teary. "He will always be my best friend." I wondered how she could say that and then leave. Which is not to say that Dad was—is—without faults. He does, however, possess infinite patience, a good share of compassion, and an overriding sense of fairness, especially with his kids.

Some years ago he raised what he thought would be a delicate subject. We were alone and he said, "I need to tell you something and I hope it won't hurt you." I braced for bad news. "When Joey was little, I promised him the ruby ring."

The ruby ring, his wedding ring, the one in his grandfather's humidor, the one I had briefly pilfered as I contemplated leaving home at age eight.

"I just wanted you to know," Dad said. "I hope you don't mind but I promised."

"That's okay, Dad. I don't mind. First you give Joey your name, then your wedding ring. It's no surprise. You've always liked him best."

He seemed stunned by the attempt at humor, as if I had turned something serious into a joke, which of course I had.

"I promised him the ring," he explained again.

Not long after, Dad began wearing another ring, one of black onyx and diamonds. It was new. "Where'd you get that?"

"Your mum got it for me. I want you to have it," he said. "Joey will get the ruby, and you'll get this one."

He's taken to wearing it on special occasions, trying to attach some sentiment to it. Decades from now after he's gone and I'm gone and one of my sons has possession of the black ring—they're still competing to determine which—they will find loads of later-in-life photos of Grandpa Joe wearing it, proof that it meant something. They might like the ring for the stone and the diamonds. But its real beauty will be in what it says about my dad.

In 1987 Northwest Flight 255 crashed outside of Detroit, killing 154 of the 155 persons on board. The lone survivor was a four-year-old named Cecelia. Initial news reports said that the girl survived because her mother had wrapped her in her arms. That was the only bright news to emerge from the tragedy: the gift of a mother's love. But that news didn't last long. Investigators determined that the girl's survival had little to do with her mother. Journalists reported the finding, correcting the earlier misinformation. Cecelia's mother had not saved her, they said.

Readers reacted angrily. What purpose, they asked, was served in dispelling an innocent myth that brought a small measure of comfort during a time of pain? Where was the harm in letting the story, inaccurate though it may be, live on? The myth was better than the harsh reality. It reassured. It offered solace. It confirmed our prettiest pictures of motherhood.

It is the work of truth tellers to separate fact from fiction and myth and legend and hoax. It is the job of journalists and historians to get the story right for posterity, and I mostly don't begrudge them that.

We know that Abner Doubleday did not invent baseball, and it seems questionable, to put it generously, whether Babe Ruth—who was not an orphan—called his shot. And there's no substantial evidence that Ty Cobb killed a man in a street fight, though the legend persists.

If we started scrutinizing our own fathers' stories and the lore that they passed to us, how well would they hold up?

Did Charlie Gehringer always watch the first pitch? Always?

Did Hal Newhouser really drive a red car—or did it just seem red to my dad's eyes?

If I went back in time to the ball field at Georgia Park, would I find my dad hitting two doubles exactly as he described them? Or was it really one? Maybe a single? Maybe a misplayed ball by the first baseman? Was Newhouser actually mad or insultingly indifferent?

And what about my childhood? And my image of my brother during Vietnam? And of Mom? And of Dad?

They got divorced after all the kids had grown and left home and after most of their grandchildren had been born, but the separation lasted only a few years and then they were living with each other again. They forged a new relationship that was stronger than the old. They had a greater appreciation for one another. Yet they never remarried, and when Mom died in 1996 they were legally, though not spiritually, separate and divided. We kids pretended that it had never happened, that they were never apart, and we let the funeral director believe that, as well as the pastor who delivered the service. The goal wasn't to deceive or mislead. Friends and relatives knew the truth. We did it for Dad because that's what he needed at the time. Or, more truthfully, was it what we needed?

Stories, like memories, serve purposes. Mostly, they confirm our view of the world—of the way things were, the way they ought to be, or the way we'd like them to be. I see now that all of the stories I tell of my father, all of the stories I've asked him to repeat over the years, the stories that I most cherish, the ones that form his legend, highlight traits that I find admirable. His Air Corps boxing lesson at the speedy hands of a flyweight points to his humility. His refusal to shoot photos of his oldest son protesting the war outside the tank plant demonstrates his love and loyalty. And his success against Hal Newhouser—the fact that he got two hits off of a guy who would later strikeout Joe DiMaggio and The Great

Ted Williams and beat Bob Feller in pitching duels—reinforces my image of him as a hero.

We all want our fathers to be our heroes.

In the museum last night, the boy in the Garciaparra jersey followed his father up the ramp that leads out the gallery. He glanced over his shoulder for a final look at the elderly ball player who had broken up Hal Newhouser's no-hitter. He thought my dad was a former major leaguer. He may even have thought him a Hall of Famer.

I've thought that myself for a long time.

26. Kirby and the Dream

In the summer of 1960, Ty Cobb, ill with cancer, came to Cooperstown for a reunion. Wrote Charles Alexander in his biography of the star, "That night after the banquet Cobb, using a cane and moving with considerable effort, walked with [Hall Director Sid] Keener from the Otesaga Hotel back to the exhibits building. They entered the Hall of Fame gallery, where Cobb stood looking at his plaque. . . . Seeing that he was wiping away tears, Keener tried to comfort him. Cobb pulled away, said only 'Good-bye,' and moved unsteadily through the exhibits and out the front door of the building." It would be his last visit. Cobb died the next year, and is interred in a mausoleum in Royston, Georgia. His sons Herschel and Ty Jr. are in a mausoleum in California with their mother.

Along Pioneer Street a parade of Yankee fans waits merrily—imagine that, if you can—in ball caps and Mantle jerseys, moving in occasional caterpillar bursts up the front slab-steps of the Tunnicliff Inn. They're mostly guys my brother's age—elderly men, in other words—and they cradle bats and balls and baseball cards and binders with photos and tubes of limited-edition prints. Their column winds through the inn's tiny lobby past the blue fireplace and the china plates on the wall toward a temporarily converted dining room in the back where for a price Whitey Ford and Yogi Berra sign their autographs.

We cut through the line and head into the hotel to gather

our luggage and check out. "There's been a cancellation if you'd like to stay another night," says the clerk.

It may seem unfathomable to other baseball fans that we would travel to Cooperstown on the cusp of Induction Weekend and not find a way to witness the gala. But we can't. I have to be home early tomorrow for a long-scheduled appearance.

Everyone says the ceremony is something to behold. If we were to stay, we might encounter Mike Shannon, founder of *Spitball* magazine, who has been coming since the 1980s and who named some of his children—Casey, Mickey, Nolan—for baseball celebrities. Or Gene Carney, better known by the pseudonym Two Finger Carney, who offers his take on the baseball world on a Web site titled "Notes from the Shadows of Cooperstown." Or Mark Schraf, a chemistry professor, who has written poems about every Hall of Fame inductee (yes, even the umpires and executives).

Then there's the event itself. The Enshrinement. For inductees nothing compares.

"Today, everything is complete," Jackie Robinson said.

"My life is fulfilled now," Lou Boudreau proclaimed.

Frankie Frisch dedicated his autobiography to the Hall of Fame. "My election to that shrine gave me my greatest baseball thrill," he wrote.

Jimmy Cobb, Ty's youngest, said his father seldom talked baseball with his sons. But he did relate his proudest achievement: being top vote getter in the first Hall of Fame election. "He used to show me the clippings where he got 211 out of a possible 214 votes"—a victory made sweeter by the fact that he beat Babe Ruth, whose company he enjoyed later in life. (How any voter could have left either man off the ballot baffles logic.)

For many, induction qualifies as the highlight of a career, which provokes an obvious question: Why is the recognition of excellent performance grander than the performance itself?

Nap Lajoie retired in 1916. There will come a time—has it arrived already?—when there is no one on this planet who saw him play in the majors. What will remain as a testament to his abilities are the statistics and the secondhand stories passed down through the generations and the accounts in books, magazines, and newspapers. And the permanent plaque—that promise of immortality—affixed to a wall in Cooperstown.

On Sunday Mazeroski and Winfield and Kirby will accept their honors, and maybe memories will trickle from their eyes. I wish we could be among the thousands who will watch.

"I'm sorry we're going to miss that," I say as we put the luggage in the van.

Dad dismisses my words with a wave of his hand.

"I don't feel like I missed anything," he says.

I've had this fantasy for a while.

It's January and I'm in Florida at one of those just-for-fun camps where baseball fans spend a week—and a fortune—playing the game and getting to know their heroes. Mickey Lolich is pitching batting practice, and Kaline and Horton are halfway paying attention as I take my swings. I drill Lolich's first three pitches over the left-field wall, and then Willie and Al get laughing and start making cracks at Lolich's expense. They watch me a little more closely. Lolich takes the ribbing good naturedly but at the same time wants to remind me who he is. He puts some speed on the ball and cuts loose a curve and then a changeup. But I'm not fooled, and now he's looking a little embarrassed and slightly pissed and he delivers a message between my chest and the inside of the plate. I slap his next one off the fence in deep left-center.

"Hey, buddy. Where'd you learn to hit?" Horton asks.

"You play in college?" Kaline wonders.

The following day I prove it's no fluke, this time against a minor leaguer who throws in the nineties. Now I really have Kaline's attention and he discreetly alerts some Tiger officials, maybe owner Mike Ilitch. "You gotta see this Stanton guy," he says. And soon I'm on my way, invited as a non-roster player to spring training where they can't cut me because I'm batting 1.000. I make the team as a designated hitter, get called to the All-Star Game, and become the talk of the major leagues, a forty-year-old *Sports Illustrated* rookie cover boy.

Until Jim Morris came along and played for Tampa Bay, it seemed pretty far-fetched. But Morris, the former high school coach, gave thousands of us renewed hope, for a short time anyway. On Sunday my aspirations will be permanently extinguished, thanks to Kirby Puckett.

Kirby is forty, born March 14, 1961. I was born December 17, 1960. He is three months younger than I, and when he gets inducted in two days he will become the first member of the Hall of Fame with a birth date more recent than mine. That's how I know my chance is gone—that and the fact that whenever I take my sons to the batting cages and get lured into the last cage to face the fastest, wildest machine I end up bunting to assure myself I can make contact. Look, I might end up at one of those fantasy camps someday, but I now grudgingly accept that I won't be playing in the major leagues.

Maybe that's the greatest difference between visiting the museum at age eleven and age forty. It's what you see. As a boy, you see your future; as a man, your past.

Main Street runs straight for several blocks. At both ends, the road bends left and the pavement disappears at the edge of town, dissolving into the hills and the horizon. Go east and you'll sweep by the Woodside Adult Residential Home. Go west and you'll pass the Victorian Gothic Otsego County Courthouse.

We turn onto Chestnut Street. It is raining and the traffic has begun to thicken coming into Cooperstown. We leave on Highway 28 with a cooler full of grapes and cookies and bottles of Coke that Dad will not drink.

Forty minutes later as we approach the I-90 entrance ramp near Herkimer, we come upon the small bridge that spans the Mohawk River. It's new and hardly merits a second look, except for its name: POW/MIA Remembrance Bridge.

We didn't notice that on the way in and my brother doesn't notice it now. Or if he does, he says nothing. But it gets me thinking.

Joey remains friends with Jim O'Connor. It was Jim's brother, Mike, a pilot, who was shot down by the Viet Cong in 1968. Every time I see Jim, I ask about Mike. Three other American soldiers died when his copter crashed. Wounded, Mike crawled through a forest for a day and a half trying to reach a pickup station where he could be rescued. When he stood to flag a U.S. helicopter, he was taken prisoner. He spent five hellish years in captivity. He served fourteen months in solitary confinement, four weeks in a grave-sized plot five feet long and two feet deep. Mike's story is one of torture endured and death witnessed, and it's not pretty. But it mesmerizes me, though I've never met him.

My brother became active in the antiwar effort in part because of Michael O'Connor's disappearance. But in the decades since, he has begun to question what he believed then and the stances he took.

"I'm glad I never had to make the decision whether to go to Canada," he has told me. "I don't think I would have gone to Vietnam, and I know I would regret it now."

"But that war was wrong," I replied.

"Sometimes," he said, "you have to make sacrifices. No one wants to but somebody has to. You have to fight for what you believe. Everybody should serve their country in some role, maybe not in the military. But there should be national service."

"That's easy to say now that you're in your forties."

"Maybe, but it's true."

I'm fascinated by the Vietnam era, and I've glorified it—and the vision of my brother within it—in a way that perhaps only a younger sibling could. For two-plus decades, I've dredged up those memories and I'm guessing that sometimes he must feel that I think his life isn't nearly as interesting as it was back then or as it could have been; that it's been a disappointment to me, that I think he should have joined the Peace Corps and made all the sacrifices that I've been unwilling to make myself. In some respects, I've sentenced him to a yearbook inscription: "Stay cool, never change."

My brother has changed, but so have I. I've worn the perm-induced curls of a Mark Fidrych mime in the 1970s and the bow ties and button-suspenders of an aspiring entrepreneur in the 1980s. I've had John-Anderson-for-President tendencies and I've spouted a few warnings about nuclear apocalypse, lest we freeze arms NOW! I've jumped the electric fence on the death penalty more than once, and for fifteen minutes wondered whether dolphins could communicate with aliens. But I would hate to have a younger brother try to define me by any of those things.

In our politics and our religion, we may never see the world the same way. Our differences are great in those areas. But, overall, we're more similar than not. And we're bonded not only by blood but by baseball.

"The tollbooth's over there," my brother says.

"Yeah, I see it."

We cross the bridge.

"You need to go west," he notes.

"Really? I thought maybe I'd drive to Boston."

27. Toward Home

When writer John McCallum drove Ty Cobb back to New York City from Cooperstown, the ball player slept much of the way. "I'm tired," he said, before dozing off. "I'm old and I'm tired. I don't like to say I'm old, but I am. . . . I've used myself up since I was seventeen. . . . Now I'm sixty-nine and I'm tired."

Utica, New York.

A blue pickup roars past us on the left, its rear window marked with a Dale Earnhardt sticker, IN MEMORY OF #3—THE INTIMIDATOR.

Oneida . . . Canastota.

We finish the last of the chocolate-coconut cookie bars that Joey's wife made.

Syracuse . . . Weedsport . . . Cayuga.

"Why would you build expensive homes like those next to an expressway?"

"I don't know," my brother says. "You mind if I take a nap?"

Seneca Falls.

ABOVE: Ty Cobb with son Ty Jr. *(Detroit Public Library, Burton Historical Collection)*

"So what are you doing this weekend, Dad?"

"Not much," he says. "Probably some yard work."

"Don't overdo it. People die from working too hard in the sun."

Clifton Springs.

"You care if I turn on the radio?"

The scanner stops for Sly and the Family Stone. "Hot fun in the summertime. . . . Ohhhh, yeah!"

Manchester . . . Victor.

My brother wakes when I hit a bump and his head slaps against the side window.

"It didn't work," I say.

"What didn't work?"

"Your beauty sleep."

We stop at a rest area for Cokes. Dad's not thirsty again. Joey drives.

Rochester . . . West Henrietta . . . Batavia.

The van in front, which we're about to pass, has a sticker. I'M FOR SOLAR ENERGY AND I VOTE, it says.

Pembroke . . . Depew . . . Buffalo.

Dad points to Dunn Tire Park on the right.

"Hurry up and eat the grapes," I tell my brother.

"Why?"

"I don't want to get waved over to customs by a border guard if she asks whether we're bringing produce into the country."

"I'm not going to eat all the grapes."

"Dad, you want some grapes?"

"Oh, a few. . . . That's enough."

There are too many grapes to eat.

"Throw them out the window."

"And get a ticket for littering?"

"It's food. It's not litter."

At Peace Bridge the guard doesn't ask about produce. As we pull away, my brother eats more grapes, and I suggest a shortcut to save a few miles near Hamilton, Ontario.

"Nah," he says. "It's going to get dark soon. I don't want to be searching for streets in some strange city."

"Wimp."

And it goes like that for most of the ride home.

It's been a special two days and we all want to preserve it and protect it, to not do anything that might sour the memory.

"Good job," my brother says when I take the correct exit ramp and merge onto 403, heading away from Toronto, not toward it.

"This doesn't look familiar."

"Umm, that's because we didn't come this way, remember?" he says.

We pass Wayne Gretzky Parkway and Wayne Gretzky Sports Center and a sign for the Canadian Baseball Hall of Fame. We stop for dinner at a place that has several fast-food options, including a Tim Hortons and a counter that sells only french fries. Fries with cheese. Fries with chili. Fries with ketchup or mustard or hot peppers or salt and vinegar. And Poutine, a French-Canadian dish of fries topped with cheese curds and thick gravy.

We go for the subs. I have almost enough Canadian money to pay for them without breaking an American twenty and getting stuck with a lot of Canadian change. I need $1.45 more.

"I've got money," my brother says.

Dad pulls out his wallet.

"No, I need Canadian money."

I check my wallet again and in a side pocket find a folded pink-and-gray two-dollar bill from 1954, the one my brother gave me when I was twelve, the souvenir from his honeymoon in Toronto.

For a brief moment, I consider spending it. Instead, I give the cashier an American twenty.

There is a sense, unspoken, that the three of us won't make this trip again. Yet it's not sadness I feel. It's fulfillment and satisfaction and joy. We've had a great time, truly memorable.

"This has been wonderful," Dad says. "I've really enjoyed it."

There doesn't need to be some greater significance to our Cooperstown trip. But it feels as if there is as we drive through the Canadian countryside into the last breaths of an orange, pink, and purple-gray sunset. There's a soothing silence, a reflective pause, with our journey nearing an end. I can feel the tires on the concrete. I can hear the truck beside us shifting down as it exits the freeway. In the rearview mirror in the darkness, I can make out parts of my father's face in shards of light: his nose—my nose; his thinning brow; an eye. He's looking out the side window at nothing in particular. "A penny for your thoughts," I should ask him but so many thoughts are coursing through my own mind.

I'm thinking of the home on Shawn Drive and how when I'm very young he sits me on the bathroom counter as he lathers his skin, dabs a bit on my cheek, and then shaves his face. It looks like he's clearing roads of snow. Then he drops the thin, flexible double-edged blade into the slit in the back of the medicine chest. "Where do they go?" I wonder.

I'm thinking of him teaching me to drive on a winter night. We're leaving a Kmart parking lot in Warren and it's icy and I'm going too fast and the Nova starts sliding sideways toward a five-lane avenue. I'm hoping he might grab the steering wheel and straighten me out. But he doesn't. "Steady," he says, and the brakes find pavement and the car stops and I feel proud because I did it myself.

I'm thinking of him later in life. He's dealing cards to Uncle Teddy and to Johnny and Rich, two of their childhood friends from the Georgia Park neighborhood. Four men, all in their seventies, sitting around a kitchen table playing pinochle. I think of him later still after Teddy, his closest older brother, has passed and how sometimes I see him wearing Teddy's Detroit Tigers ball cap.

I'm thinking of the first time I felt he really needed me.

Mom was dying. She had cancer of the brain and bone. It was after Thanksgiving in 1996 and she was sitting in her hospital bed in a room the color of lilacs and pussy willows. She was just being Mom, normal in all respects except one. She kept talking about how she had been unable to sleep the night before because a baby had been crying. I was thinking that maybe a friend of a nurse had dropped by with a child or that there was an emergency in the cancer ward and that a whole family, baby and all, had ended up on the floor.

"I'll talk to the nurse about it, Mom."

"The nurse don't believe me," she said, scowling. "They brought the baby through the wall. There's a secret door they open at night."

She motioned toward a solid wall. Dad was seated in front of it, trying to keep his smile. The voice was Mom's. The inflections were right. She didn't sound crazy. She was telling us this as she would tell us anything. "The baby was crying and they brought the baby in my room. There were cats jumping on my bed. I couldn't sleep with all that racket."

She looked at me to gauge whose side I was on. Did I believe the nurse or did I believe her? Would I believe my own mother's story?

"That's what happened," she said. "There's a door that opens at night and the doctor brings the baby out." She paused and squinted at me. "Well, I can tell you don't believe me."

I struggled for words.

"No, I believe you, Mom. I'm just thinking . . . um . . . they . . . they shouldn't be bringing a baby into your room."

"Well, they did, and I was holding the baby and trying to make the baby stop crying. But there were cats jumping on the bed. I don't like cats, and I don't feel good enough to take care of a baby. I just wish I could get some sleep."

A few nights later after Mom had undergone emergency surgery, Joey, Dad, and I stood in the hospital parking lot, about to get into our own cars. Snow drifted through the yellowish streetlights. It had been a rough day, and the prognosis looked poor.

Dad, who had been so strong in the hospital room beside Mom, finally broke down. They had moved Mom from the cancer ward to the intensive care unit. They had emptied her drawers and put her clothes into a plastic bag with handles, the kind you carry home.

"A plastic bag," he said outside in the cold. He was angry and hurt. His eyes glistened, his voice weakened. "Someone as important as your mother and they put her clothes in a plastic bag." He looked at us as if we could explain.

My dad is in the backseat.

I'm forty. I've advanced from Tang to orange-flavored Metamucil and can do a convincing job acting adult. But in some ways I'm still that kid bouncing around on the sidewalk out front in the shade of the birch tree as my dad and brother throw the baseball back and forth and I demand their attention, pursue their praise, and hope for the approval that no matter how abundant never quite fills me up. I do it more subtly now by inviting them to see me at the Hall of Fame. But when you pare it down, there is that element to it and I'm not sure I'll ever entirely outgrow it. That need to impress them has been responsible for a lot of overachievement in my life.

My dad knows it. Earlier today while my brother was in the museum gift shop, Dad and I were looking at a painting of Ty Cobb in his baggy uniform, a round glove on his hand. Dad lightly batted his fingers against my arm to get my attention. His face was serious, his eyes piercing into mine. "I'm really proud of you," he said. But the way he spoke—firmly, unequivocally, infused with fatherly authority—conveyed something deeper. I heard it this way: "I'm really proud of you, I've always been proud of you, and I'll continue to be proud of you no matter what's on your resume. Now, please stop trying so hard."

He said it as if it were the most important thing he would ever tell me.

I almost made a joke to lighten the moment.

As he gets on into his eighties, he's tying together the loose ends of his life. He begins sentences with these words, "I plan to be here for another seven or eight years but just in case I think you should know . . ." and then he tells us what arrangements he's made for Mom's cottage up north or how many years are left on his car's lease or in whose name he has put his savings account.

I can't imagine my life without him.

There's been a subtle transition underway since Mom died five years ago, and it feels as if it's being formalized on this trip—the only overnight trip the three of us have taken together.

The ball players aren't the only men being inducted this weekend.

It would be an exaggeration to say we could not have come to Cooperstown before now, to imply that Wee Willie Keeler and Kenesaw Mountain Landis and Charlie Gehringer and "Moonlight" Graham had somehow conspired to delay a boyhood dream to give our present journey greater significance. We could have found a way but did not. After that summer of 1972 I never pestered my father about the Hall of Fame, not with the same persistence or intensity. The topic arose occasionally, primarily in winter when newspapers carried stories of the elections of Spahn, Mantle, and Whitey Ford, or when Harwell or Garagiola shared an anecdote about the place.

By the mid-1970s I was in high school and bemoaning any talk of a long trip that might confine me to a car with my father. By my teenage sensibilities, he had grown almost unbearable, and I no longer hungered for his stories about Gehringer and Greenberg. They had temporarily lost their luster.

In 1980 Al Kaline got elected on the first ballot. It was a big deal in Michigan where children of three decades had grown up worshipping him. Dad and I watched the news coverage as Kaline's voice cracked. Dad was sixty, still working at the tank arsenal. Colleen was in high school. "We should go to the Hall of Fame one of these days," he said. "We've been talking about it a long time."

"Yeah, that'd be nice, Dad."

But I was approaching my twentieth birthday, commuting to college, working as a newspaper reporter, hanging out with friends, and discovering a woman with eyes as blue as Tiffany glass. Baseball, like Dad, had been relegated to a supporting role.

It happens if you're a fan long enough. You have years where the sport's hold on you weakens. It might have something to do with the game—your team's lousy performance, the trade of a favorite player, a strike—but more likely it's just the circumstances of your life, possibly the arrival of those teenage years when girls become suddenly more intriguing or that stage after high school when the world opens before you as a panorama of possibilities and everything you once cherished fades beside your new discoveries.

Beth and I married in 1983, and our three boys arrived in the five years that followed. That decade and much of the next brought a whirl of activity—family, school, career—that never slowed. I often promised myself that someday I'd go to the Hall of Fame with my sons, someday "when they get older, when they can appreciate it." Someday.

Perhaps you have your own somedays.

Well, my boys got older, into junior and senior high, and though they would have politely accompanied me on the journey, none of them really yearned to visit Cooperstown. But my brother and my father still did, and there's something perfect about that, isn't there? Something perfect about linking the circle, about going to baseball's ultimate destination with the two people who introduced you to the sport, the two who sparked that dream so many seasons past.

Really, isn't that what it's about for most who make the trip: completing a circle? Isn't that what it's about for Rudy Gafur, dreaming of baseball in America while growing up in Guyana? And for Harold Gach, in the final days of his life, thinking of games at the ballpark with his late father and, decades on, his son? And for the ball players awaiting enshrinement? And for the tens of thousands who come each year, some as old men revisiting their heroes, some as young fathers hoping to inspire in their children the love for the game that their own dads instilled in them.

The road to Cooperstown looks different for all of us. But no matter what route we've taken—metaphorically in life or literally on pavement—it leads us to the same place, back to where it began for most of us, back to our childhoods. And that's fitting.

Because baseballs are round, after all, and they have raised red stitches that look like arrows and point you along a seam that if followed will return you to where you started.

Tom," says my brother Joe as we drive through Canada, "isn't the ball game on the radio?"

We find Ernie Harwell's broadcast. The Tigers are playing the A's, and the game is tied 1-1 in the late innings, and Jeff Weaver is facing Jason Giambi. But it could just as easily be Mickey Lolich and Reggie Jackson. Or even Schoolboy Rowe and Jimmie Foxx.

Acknowledgments

Many good people helped this book along the way.

For his sound advice and unwavering support, I thank my agent, Philip Spitzer, and for his timely encouragement and perceptive guidance, my editor Pete Wolverton, associate publisher of Thomas Dunne Books.

At the National Baseball Hall of Fame, Dale Petroskey, Scot Mondore, Bruce Markusen, and, especially, Tim Wiles provided invaluable assistance. At Thomas Dunne Books, Joe Rinaldi, John Parsley, and Harriet Seltzer extended various courtesies, as did W. C. Burdick, Russell Wolinsky, and Rachael Kepner of the Hall of Fame Library and David Poremba of the Detroit Public Library. Others who graciously contributed expertise, advice, and memories include Ed Rychlewski, Jim O'Connor, Connie Stanton, Colleen and Michael Rudi, Janis Stanton, Cliff Kachline, Tom Heitz, Ted Hathaway of Rational Pastimes, Adele Johnson of the Fenimore Museum Library, Susan Perkins of the Herkimer County Historical

Society, Mike Varney, Rob Edelman, Gene Carney, Bobby Plapinger, Mark Schraf, Mike Wowk, Judith Wainscott, copyeditor Sean O. Perruzzi, and Tim Morris. The 1972 reporting of Mitch Kehetian of the *Macomb Daily*, Jim Hawkins and Joe Falls of the *Detroit Free Press*, Larry Paladino of the Associated Press, and Watson Spoelstra of the *Detroit News* also shaped this story. In addition, I thank my childhood friend Jeff Mancini, with whom I reconnected in the autumn of 2002.

Above and beyond all else, I deeply appreciate the support of my wife, Beth Bagley-Stanton, who read various drafts; my sons, Zachary, William, and Taylor, who inspired the work; and, in particular, my father, Joseph Stanton, and my brother, Joseph Stanton Jr., who allowed their lives to be explored on these pages.

About the Author

Tom Stanton is the author of *The Final Season,* which won the Casey Award for Best Baseball Book of the Year. A journalist for twenty-five years, Stanton was the recipient of a Michigan Journalism Fellowship. A former assistant professor at the University of Detroit Mercy, he lives in New Baltimore, Michigan, with his wife, Beth, and their three sons. He may be reached at www.tomstanton.com.